a. Douglas; ☑ **W9-CRW-838**

NO DANCING GOD
MENNONITE STORIES

Canadian Cataloguing in Publication Data

Driediger, Ab Douglas

ISBN 1-55056-615-6
1. Mennonites – Ethnic Identity – Mennonites Autobiograghy,
   Biography, Short Stories.

Rutgers Publications
201-634 Lequime Rd
Kelowna BC V1W 1A4
250-764-8745

Printed in Canada by Friesens

NO DANCING
GOD

STORIES ON A MENNONITE THEME

~ CONTENTS ~

ABOUT THE AUTHOR

Ab (Douglas) Driediger was born in Mölln, Germany into a Mennonite family enroute to Canada from Russia, and grew up in south western Manitoba.

He is a graduate of the Winkler Collegiate Institute, and took his BA (Political Science) from Queen's University in Kingston, Ontario.

He began a career in broadcast journalism in 1951, under the name Ab Douglas, working in several newsrooms in the Prairies before joining the CTV news team in Ottawa in 1962, where he was Parliamentary Bureau Chief and co-anchor of the National News with Peter Jennings (now with ABC).

In 1967, he moved to CBC working as a documentaries producer in Toronto, a national reporter in Alberta and British Columbia and foreign correspondent in Moscow, as well as other overseas locations.

In 1980, he left the CBC for a teaching position at the University of Regina's School of Journalism.

Since 1984, his time has been taken up with his own media consulting business, writing, and looking after his horses and cattle on a farm near Medicine Hat, Alberta.

Also by the author
On Foreign Assignment
The Inside Story of Journalism's Elite Corps

Three of the stories in this book have been previously published.
Honourable Men All appeared in the University of Winnipeg's Journal of Mennonite Studies.
Be a Gooda Boy and *The Germans are Coming....The Germans are Coming* in Green's Magazine.

Credits
Book production and design Back Forty Publications Medicine Hat, AB
Graphics and photo consultant Barbara Heinrich
Manuscript typing Debbie Kendall

This book is dedicated to my brother and sisters

I would believe only in a God
who could dance. And when I
saw my devil I found him
serious,
thorough, profound, and solemn:
it was the spirit of
gravity — through him all things
fall. Not by wrath does one kill
but by laughter. Come, let us
kill the spirit of gravity!

- Friedrich Nietzsche

Introduction

The stories in this book hover in the twilight zone between reality and fiction. Some are autobiographical in nature and others biographical. Still others have been endowed with a high degree of flexibility in order to illuminate moral and emotional values and achieve "poetical truths". Even these are, in most instances, drawn from actual events and real people.

What I have striven for is, to paraphrase Robert Graves, a nice contradiction between fact and fiction to make the whole read human and exact.

A Sense of Place and Time sets the stage for the stories that follow, and is essentially an assemblage of personal recollections of a particular time and place in the life of one community of Mennonites uprooted from the steppes of Russia to begin a new and, at times, bewildering life on the Canadian prairies. The time of the stories ranges from the desperate 30's, the war years, to the budding prosperity of the 50's.

I have taken the liberty of changing proper names to avoid hurting the feelings of the living and distressing the dead. Characterization is, however, as accurate as I could possibly make it.

While the stories do unearth old, and not so old, Mennonite vices, I hope the reader will find at least a few glimpses of virtues, of which there are many ." What our people strove to be is as important as what they actually were." It is my hope that everyone, regardless of ethnicity, will find at least a part of his, or her, own story in the biography of others; maybe a shock of recognition, perhaps a wistful smile of nostalgia.

Without a story you cannot have a place or a people

— *Sir Laurens Van der Post*

A SENSE OF PLACE AND TIME

As prairie towns went, there was nothing unusual or extraordinary about Kirkcaldy. There were a thousand towns just like it scattered across the relentless landscape. On a map they looked like strings of beads strung together by a network of threads which seemed at one and the same time to lead everywhere and nowhere.

These were the branchlines of the Canadian Pacific and Canadian National railways linking the communities with one another and the outside world ... a world into which few ventured except when young men were summoned to defend King and Country, and young women travelled to faraway cities to train as nurses or work as domestics. Kirkcaldy was on a CPR branchline.

There was also a gravel road that ran 17 miles due south, connecting with a slightly wider gravel road called the Number One or Trans Canada Highway. A right-hand turn at this junction and a five hour dust or mud-churning drive, depending on the weather, brought the intrepid motorist to Regina. A turn to the left, and a hundred miles on somewhat better gravel led to Brandon.

The towns were built about seven miles apart so a grain elevator was within easy reach of any farmer with a sturdy wagon and a strong team of Belgians or Clydesdales.

Most towns had more than one elevator, usually two, sometimes three, occasionally four and rarely five. The greater the number of elevators that broke the prairie skyline, the higher the town rated on the area's economic and cultural scale. Kirkcaldy was a two elevator town.

It was laid out in the shape of a capital T. The top of the T paralleled the railway and was, of course, called Railway Avenue. At least that is the designation it was given on the official map hanging in the Municipal Office. The townspeople and area farmers didn't call it anything. The T's stem was called Ellice Street on the map. Except for Franklin Bellamy, the municipal secretary, no one knew or cared that that street had a name either.

Together, Railway Avenue and Ellice Street embraced the business axis into which the town's few residential streets led. Each street, or dirt road, was edged with snaggle-toothed rows of clapboard houses, each with an outhouse in the back yard. The more genteel folks referred to them as toilets, or privies. Most everyone else called them backhouses, although the town toughs, who took a perverse delight in tipping them over on Halloween night, had an even less elegant name for them.

All the essentials, but little more, were to be found in the business establishments on Railway and Ellice. At Bannister's General Store farm wives looked over gingham for their daughters' dresses and bib overalls for the men and boys, but usually ended up ordering from the T. Eaton Company catalog where everything was so much cheaper.

On Saturday nights, farmers gathered in town to gossip and admire the latest lines of farm machinery at the Massey Harris and John Deere dealers'. There was a lot of looking and little buying.

After quietly debating the merits and shortcomings of each machine they sauntered over to get in line for a haircut at Whit Walton's barber shop. In spite of the musical rhyme, "shave and a haircut ... two bits," a shave was ten cents extra.

At the south end of Railway Avenue stood the granary-sized Manitoba Government Telephone Exchange where Vi Proudfoot plugged in and unplugged a bewildering array of jacks dangling at the end of insulated cords. These could theoretically put Vi, and by extension all of Kirkcaldy, in touch with places with big-sounding names like Winnipeg, Toronto, New York and Chicago. Maybe even London and Paris if there hadn't been a war going on.

With all this power at their fingertips, Vi and her relief operator were considered to have the most glamorous jobs in town and, next to the school teachers were the most desirable catches for bachelor farmers. At least Vi was. Her assistant, although attractive, was another matter. At eighteen, she was a child in a woman's body, full-lipped with a bubbly personality and an easy smile. One of the women at the Ladies' Aid meeting was once heard to remark that she was "too generous" with her affection! In spite of that, or perhaps because of it, she never lacked for a date to take her to the dances at the Odd

Fellows Hall. Yet the whole time she was in Kirkcaldy, not a single marriage proposal, and in time, she became known derisively among the boys as "Switchboard Sally."

Nevertheless, Sally turned out alright in the end. She moved to Brandon where she met and married a young pilot, recently discharged from the airforce. Folks said he'd flown Spitfires in the Battle of Britain, but it was just a rumour. What wasn't a rumour was that his father owned the city's largest Ford dealership.

Sally and her husband moved into a large yellow brick house in the good part of town and started raising a family. She was elected president of the Junior League and her picture appeared regularly in the Brandon Sun's society pages, clippings of which her mother proudly passed around at the Ladies' Aid meetings back in Kirkcaldy.

Few farms had phones, so anxious mothers came to the telephone office to make long distance calls to daughters in Brandon who had gone to work as domestics, waitresses or nurses aides. They left home to get away from the back breaking farm work; from having to milk ten or more cows by hand twice a day. They left to escape small town boredom. They left, like Sally, to escape vicious gossip. Like all small towns, Kirkcaldy always lay in wait for the scent of scandal, one false step around which to circle like screeching sea gulls eyeing a scrap of garbage.

As often as not, these phone conversations sounded like one way shouting matches, the conventional wisdom being that the farther the voice had to travel along the telephone wires, the greater the need to speak louder. The conversations were usually timed to precisely three minutes to avoid extra charges. The mothers would emerge from the phone booth flushed and perspiring ... sometimes dabbing their eyes with a crumpled handkerchief. Their verdict on the vagaries of the communications technology of the day invariable took two forms: "My, she sounded just like she was in the next room. Clear as a bell." Or, "there was so much noise I could hardly make out a word."

Over at the Chinese Cafe at the extreme north end of Railway, every kid from miles around was taking his turn at the ice cream counter. The Chinaman is what the grownups called the Chinese gentleman who ran the cafe. It was located on the ground floor of the two-storey yellow brick Odd Fellows Hall. He lived alone, and as far as anyone knew, had no wife or children back in China. To the children, who were his most avid patrons, he was known simply as Charlie. To the macho older boys he was the "Chink."

No one knew his real name, nor cared, except perhaps Mr. Bellamy. Every Christmas Charlie would send Mrs. Bellamy an intricately embroidered Chinese handkerchief and order in several bricks of metropolitan ice cream from Brandon for the town's first family.

Wild rumours about Charlie circulated. One was that any stray dog or cat stood a pretty good chance of ending up on Charlie's menu. Another, and the more persistent, was that he kept a stash of extraordinarily long knives at the back of his cafe, and that he'd been known to throw these at complaining customers. Credible evidence of such an incident ever having occurred was never produced, but such a minor detail failed to dampen the wild stories. Probably the worst offence that Charlie ever committed was selling nickel packs of Turret cigarettes to young boys.

The rumours made absolutely no impression on the youngsters clutching their Saturday dime pondering the choice of ice cream flavors. Patiently Charlie would recite the three available which never varied from one week to the next: "wahrnuh, vanirah and slawbelly."

While Charlie rented the ground floor of the Odd Fellows Hall, he was of course not a member. Nor did he attend any of the community events held upstairs or anywhere else in town. The building he shared with the Odd Fellows had been the grandest in town until the two-storey red brick four-room school opened in 1916. The school was the only structure for miles around that boasted running water and indoor toilets. Two outhouses were nevertheless built on the grounds as backup in case the plumbing froze, which it frequently did.

In spite of the new school, the Odd Fellows Hall retained its status as the community's cultural centre and gathering place. It was here that the Chautauqua performances had once been held. Kirkcaldy had been on the Chautauqua circuit, albeit the second string circuit, before and during the First World War and a few years after. Authors, politicians and explorers came to lecture and enlighten. Musicians, actors and vaudeville performers came to entertain. Had Kirkcaldy been on the A circuit, like some of the larger centres, professional theatre companies would have come to stage such popular plays as *School For Scandal*. But by the time the Dirty Thirties hit, Chautauqua was but a distant memory. Radios were scarce, and entertainment, if there was to be any, had to be homemade.

There were Christmas Tree concerts, (at which each teacher was judged by the performance of her students), dances and whist drives. From time to time missionaries arrived with boxes full of slides showing dark skinned people with dazzling white smiles who, the missionaries solemnly declared, had been brought to the Lord.

The John Deere movies were the biggest hit. School kids got the afternoon off to see them. Sure, they had to sit through the reel extolling the excellence of the John Deere Company's farm machinery, but then came the slightly ancient newsreels and a rip roaring comedy.

The comedy always had a rural setting and without fail there was a city slicker who somehow ended up on a farm doing all kinds of stupid things like picking up the wrong crate at the railway station. Instead of bringing the farmer the milking machine he'd ordered, he loaded the curling machine intended for Myrtle's Hair Salon. Of course every farmer in the place knew what was coming. The ladies at Myrtle's got their hair pulled and the cows all sported curled teats. For the country folk it was all a vicarious way of getting even with their city cousins who, they felt, tended to view them as dim-witted rubes.

Laughs were hard to come by. 1937 was a particularly tough year. It brought a drought the likes of which the prairies had never seen. Hot winds seared an already parched landscape blowing top soil into five foot drifts completely burying fence posts. Dark, distant clouds talked of rain but nearly always broke their promise. Grasshoppers came in sky-darkening swarms to devour the few blades of crop that managed to survive. And when they were finished with that, they moved into the pastures and chewed up the grass.

The winter was severe too. Farmers, whose pride had never allowed them to take a handout, pulled their teams and sleighs up along the CPR siding to load up boxes of dried cod from Newfoundland and small hard apples from British Columbia. "Wouldn't be taking this if it wasn't for the kids," they'd say.

It was during this hard year that Miss Rachel Portman, one of the most conscientious teachers Kirkcaldy had ever had, lifted everyone's spirits by staging a comic operetta. It was called *Green Cheese*, and was such a smash hit at home that it went on the road touring several of the neighboring communities. It got rave reviews in the World News & Spectator, the local paper.

All these events, and later the Victory Bond rallies, were held in the Odd Fellows Hall. Each event, no matter how minor, was brought to a dramatic conclusion with the rolling down of a canvas stage curtain. On the side facing the audience was a huge painting of a mountain scene. A majestic elk stood in the middle of a stream of blue glacial water, the likes of which could only be dreamt of on the prairies. Once the curtain was down, everyone stood stiffly to attention and belted out an off-key version of *God Save the King*, all the while staring straight ahead into the elk's eye.

Kirkcaldyites were, if nothing else, patriotic proud sons and daughters of the Empire. The Union Jack snapped smartly in the prairie wind above the school and municipal office. On the First of July and on Armistice Day veterans of the "Great War" draped the flag inside screened verandas. In the classroom, Miss Portman added new wartime songs to her rather tired repertoire of old English folk tunes. Songs like, *There'll Always Be An England, Land of Hope and Glory* and *Comin' In On A Wing And A Prayer* gave the old standard *Pack Up Your Troubles* a well earned rest.

Miss Portman was a spinster. Her fiance had been killed in the First World War. As far as anyone knew, she had never again shown the slightest interest in another man. She was a sensible woman. She used no makeup, wore her steel gray hair in a short bob and had a preference for plainly cut navy blue dresses. She wore sensible square heeled "nurses" shoes. These were available from Eaton's catalog in black or white. Their only concession to frivolity were tiny leather tassels that hung from the instep.

When she bent over a desk to cast a critical glance at an exercise book, eyebrows raised to peer over her wire-rimmed glasses, there was the unmistakable scent of ... not perfume ... but the sensible fragrance of Yardley lavender soap.

As might be expected, her classes were the most disciplined in the school. She brooked no nonsense. With one withering look she instilled the fear of God in every student, not to mention the other teachers.

Miss Portman was, what one might call, fastidious when it came to personal hygiene. She tirelessly tried to impress upon her charges, especially the boys, to make regular contact with soap and water.

The farm boys' lack of attention to such nuisances and the inevitable residue of cow manure on boots created an aroma in the well heated classrooms that was usually enough to overwhelm Miss Portman's Yardley soap. In late fall this redolence was often enhanced by the distinct smell of animal musk as boys who had checked their traplines before school had forgotten to remove a dead weasel or two from their back overall pocket.

In spite of the odds, she incessantly drilled the accepted verities of the day into the heads of her students; "a stitch in time ..." "waste not want not". "Cleanliness is next to godliness" was one she had cause to draw on most frequently.

She realized that water was a scarce commodity on the prairies during those dry years. The solution, she would say, was the sponge bath. Simply put a small dipper full of water in a basin, wet a wash cloth and dab it over the entire body. This daily chore, she said, would tide everyone over from one Saturday bath to the next. She of course made the reckless assumption that her students in fact took regular Saturday baths.

The First World War forever changed Miss Portman's life and it took a heavy toll on all of Kirkcaldy. Its young men had answered the call to arms without the slightest hesitation. In the words of one newspaper, "they were inspired from the very commencement of hostilities by patriotic devotion, and offered themselves as one for the service of the flag." If there was any questioning about the rights and wrongs of that war, and what had actually been achieved at such heavy cost, it was done in the solitude of a grieving heart.

The absence of so many young men created a vacuum in the

countryside. Elderly farmers who couldn't carry on without their sons moved into town. Many of the veterans who made it back were broken in health, and unable to resume farming. Others, who had seen the bright lights of the big cities, could not face the prospect of resuming their hum drum pre-war life. There was a lot of truth in the Irving Berlin song...."How'r ya gonna keep 'em down on the farm after they've seen Pah-ree." The upshot was that there was a lot of loose land lying around that could be had for a song. It was snapped up by a few enterprising local businessmen.

The war had been good to them. Not only were they able to accumulate large land holdings, the Russian Revolution that came in the war's wake, brought another unexpected windfall. Thousands of ethnic German Mennonite farmers who had lost their land under Communist collectivization were coming to Canada in ever increasing numbers. They were exactly the kind of people Kirkcaldy's new land entrepreneurs were looking for to till their newly acquired fields.

Twelve Mennonite families, uprooted from the fertile soil of Ukraine and the Siberian steppes by the tidal wave of war and revolution came to Kirkcaldy as sharecroppers. They had left behind prosperous farms, well built homes, and in some cases large estates staffed by Russian peasant servants. Their lives had been self contained, insular and homogenous. They had run their own schools in the German language, operated their own hospitals and other community institutions and worshiped as their faith decreed in their own churches. For the first time in their lives they would have to mix with another culture with different mores and values. They would have to live with, what the Mennonites called, the "English." They would have to learn the English language. (Few had bothered to learn Russian in their former homeland). They would have to send their children to English schools. (None had ever allowed their children to attend Russian schools). There was one thing, however, on which they would not compromise...nor were they ever asked to. They continued to worship in the faith that had sustained them for more than four centuries, first in Holland, then Germany and later under the czars. They met for Sunday services in private homes and invited the ministers from Winnipeg to baptize their sons and daughters.

12

They were excellent farmers. The Kirkcaldy land owners were happy to have them as tenants, and the Mennonites were grateful to be given a chance to start a new life in a new land. This gratitude inhibited them from ever mentioning publicly that Kirkcaldy had not been their first choice. They would have preferred to settle among their own in the West and East Reserves near Winnipeg in the southern part of the province.

That area had been settled by Mennonites in the late 1800's and early 1900's. There, this people apart, lived much as they had in the Old Country, in farm villages with barns an extension of the house, and cattle pastured communally.

Although children were obliged to be taught English in school, German and religious classes were held either during or after regular school hours. Once out of the classrooms, the children reverted to the low German dialect and just as automatically switched to High German for Sunday church services.

This is where Kirkcaldy's Mennonites, and thousands like them, would have liked to settle, but they were too late. By the time they decided to leave what was by the mid-twenties the Soviet Union, the black-loamed plains of the West Reserve around Winkler were taken. Even the scrubby, stony East Reserve around Steinbach was fully settled by earlier Mennonite migrants.

This isolation from their own kind brought about an enforced integration with a predominantly Anglo Saxon community. It was only achieved with time and after a war that brought with it painful racial discrimination. Yet, no one regretted coming. Their land in Russia, whether large holdings or small, had been confiscated. Month by month the little news that filtered out from behind the Iron Curtain (a phrase coined by Sir Winston Churchill 20 years after it had become a reality) was grim. There were crop failures and famine on a massive scale. The farms on which Mennonite farmers had prospered for over a century, and which had made Russia a world class wheat exporter, were neglected and experiencing one crop failure after another. Grain was being expropriated. Even worse, Mennonite ministers were being executed and their young men were banished to slave labour camps in the limitless reaches of Siberia.

No matter how hard life was on the Canadian prairie...drought, depression, grasshoppers or dust storms, the pious Mennonites gathered every Sunday to thank God for deliverance and the new found freedom to worship in their own way in a new land.

The Mennonites were industrious introverts. Their rented farms were neat and tidy. Yards were raked, old machinery was neatly lined up and kept in as good a working condition as its age and money allowed. Landlords spent no money on paint or building repairs, so houses and barns stood grey and weather beaten against the stark horizon. As if to compensate for this drabness, the women surrounded their homes with a profusion of flowers, a kaleidoscopic explosion of reds, whites, yellows and oranges; of hollyhocks, nasturtiums, marigolds, zinnias and gladioli. Behind these huge flowerbeds every foot of ground was broken up for raspberries, gooseberries, and strawberries and a complete catalog of every fruit and vegetable suitable to be grown during the short prairie summers, and a few that were not.

Yes, the Mennonites were an agricultural people. The love of the land was next to love of God himself in giving purpose to life on this earth. Their children (usually many) were a special gift from the Lord to be reared as God-fearing Christians who would (thanks to the infallibility of the Mennonite faith) be saved from the eternal fires of damnation and eventually be called to the heavenly throne of God to hear His benediction of life everlasting..."well done thou good and faithful servant."

In the meantime, until death or marriage intervened, Mennonite boys and girls were the uncomplaining servants of their earthly father. They were cheap and abundant labor in the fields, gardens and milk sheds. Young boys of seven or eight felt the sting of horse urine on their bare chapped feet while cleaning out stables. Shoes were to be worn only on Sundays or when an itinerant preacher came to call. The sunburned paternal hand that held the well worn family Bible was the same hand that brought a leather martingale down on a young boy's back with lacerating force. The offence was usually minor and as often as not, non existent.

It was a grim theology. Fun wasn't a sin as long as there wasn't too much of it all at one time. Singing was encouraged if the

14

songs were hymns or of a gospel nature. Dancing, playing cards, fashionable clothes, movies and most other forms of entertainment were forbidden. Children were constantly reminded that although they were in the world, they were not of the world. (Miss Portman's Green Cheese operetta was definitely out).

The world encroached nevertheless. Innocently at first. The more erudite of the Mennonite children devoured the juvenile classics; *Treasure Island, Swiss Family Robinson* and *Anne of Green Gables*. Parents didn't favor the school's reading curriculum, but set aside their aversion to fiction which, they reasoned, was made up and was thus not true. By logical extrapolation it was therefore a lie.

In fairness, the Kirkcaldy Mennonites did not scorn learning as long as there wasn't too much of it. A basic competence in the three R's was considered quite sufficient to get anyone through life. This translated into a Grade 8 education. The Mennonites' concern was not so much that their children were being taught but what they were being taught with the result that a university education was either strenuously discouraged or grudgingly allowed. Old man Thiessen didn't have enough land for all his boys, so he sent his youngest off to college. Claimed that after that he couldn't get a straight answer out of the kid. The worry was that higher learning would contaminate young souls with socialist doctrine, and theories that humans evolved from monkeys. There certainly was no danger of intellectual corruption in the local school.

Kirkcaldy was no hotbed of revolutionary agitation or evolutionary thought. The few books that existed in the community were deposited in the sparse school library, and would have rested there largely undisturbed if Miss Portman had not insisted on a five book a year reading quota. Music education was what she pounded out on the school's Bell piano with students from all grades joining in on lusty sing alongs with old English folk tunes like, *John Peel* and *Men of Harlech*. Thin gruel indeed to whet the intellectual appetite.

Kirkcaldy was, in spite of the valiant efforts of some, a stagnant cultural backwater. The smattering of seedlings that threw out roots in its unpromising soil had to be transplanted to grow and mature elsewhere.

Mental images of that "elsewhere" were plucked out of the ether on the radio. By the time war broke out in 1939 most homes had this miraculous invention in their kitchens or living rooms. The novelty of temperamental crystal sets with earphones had been replaced by more dependable battery operated mantle radios with built-in speakers. For some time the Mennonites resisted this worldly intrusion into their lives. But pleading and cajoling by the children brought on a capitulation of sorts. How, the children argued, could the radio be the devil's instrument when there were all those evangelists on the American stations preaching salvation? And, during the week there were the news bulletins, weather reports and the CBC farm broadcasts from Winnipeg. Surely no one could argue that these programs were not worthwhile...and safe.

At the beginning there was strict censorship, but as the novelty wore off a grudging tolerance for other programs set in...IF the volume was kept low.

For the younger set no evening was complete without the Lone Ranger's shout of "Hi ho Silver" accompanied by Rossini's thundering overture from William Tell. There was the Chicago Symphony on WGN...puzzling music one Mennonite housewife called it. Music, she said, that had no definite beginning and no end, and in which every musician wandered about on his own, with the result that the tunes never seemed to lead anywhere.

The Mormon Tabernacle choir on KSL Salt Lake City was another matter. Like a clap of thunder the Tabernacle's great pipe organ launched into *A Mighty Fortress is Our God*. Almost simultaneously the choir would join in with uncompromising authority and with the finality of the last judgment. Now that, according to the older folks, was real music, and whoever happened to be sitting closest to the radio could confidently turn up the volume without the slightest fear of reproach. Even the hint of Catholic heresy implicit in *Ave Maria* was overlooked. No one stirred until the pianissimo amen had faded out. The Mormon's rewriting of the words replacing the "Ave Maria" with "heavenly father" met with quiet approval from the staunchly Protestant anabaptist Mennonites.

By the time spring seeding rolled around, both the dry B's and the wet A car battery had run down from heavy winter use and

16

the radio went into a kind of summer hibernation. (There was no power on farms). Farm work expanded to fill the long daylight hours leaving little time to indulge in any frivolities like listening to the radio.

Left long enough though, the batteries revived enough to pick up a weepy evangelist on the Fargo station on Sundays. But programs with no redeeming features, like the *Lone Ranger*, *Boston Blackie* and the *Green Hornet*, would have to wait for freeze up. Then, a new set of large Eveready B batteries and a fully recharged car battery would be hooked up for another winter's entertainment. Outside, the 40 foot aerial would be checked for summer storm damage and everything was set to pull in stations from as far away as Amarillo, Texas on a good night. Another cycle of life on a prairie Mennonite farm was about the begin.

For the Kirkcaldy Mennonites that included drawing spiritual inspiration and sustenance from the schizophrenic theology of the American radio evangelists. They dispensed a mixture of salvation and hucksterism that seemed to be accepted without question, while the churches of the English community were rejected as heretical and false.

United Churches were as much a part of the prairie landscape as grain elevators. Like most, Kirkcaldy's was a white wooden structure with clear glass windows. While the crab grass and weeds grew suspiciously high around the Anglican Church, the United was well attended and its minister recognized as a pillar of the community.

The puritanical rigidity of the Methodists and Presbyterians had mellowed over the years since the melding of the two denominations into the United Church of Canada. Nevertheless, the uncompromising moral strictures held by these stern forebears remained embedded in the statute books. A bylaw forbade anyone from indecently exposing themselves in any street or public place within the limits of the rural municipality. This was fine as far as it went, but the law further stipulated that, "the call of nature shall not be any palliation of the offence." For a town without a single public facility (the Ladies' Aid restrooms were to come later), it was a harsh law indeed. No one, with the possible exception of Franklin Bellamy, knew that such a law existed. As a result, flagrant and frequent violations took place behind the hedges of the empty lot back of Cleetis Jones' livery stable.

The bylaws covered pretty well all the pit falls into which human frailty might lead, and then some. Bawdy houses were of course outlawed, but so was swimming in ponds and ditches along roadsides during daylight hours.

There was no beer parlour in Kirkcaldy. Those who took an occasional drink did so most discreetly. Two citizens who took more than an occasional drink, and not discreetly, were Big Bob Murdoch and Daddy Joe Burns. They were the town drunks, and made their own booze in a bluff near the dump. Whenever their long suffering wives thought matters were getting out of hand, they would follow a well worn path into the dense poplar and willow growth and take an axe to the still. They would do so just before a new batch of home brew was almost ready to go on stream.

Well, Big Bob and Daddy Joe may have been deadbeats who couldn't provide for their families, but they were also mechanical geniuses. In no time they were back in business beating a new path to another hideaway.

Those who just went on sporadic binges would drive down the road about 15 miles to the "licensed premises" in St. Lambert. It was a French Canadian town, and it was as Catholic as Kirkcaldy was Protestant. While the Kirkcaldyites readily conceded that the French folks of St. Lambert did not worship a lesser God than they, He was nevertheless a much looser God. This in no way discouraged the leading Protestant families from sending their nubile daughters to take their final years of high school behind the protective walls of St. Lambert's convent.

These same families, if they imbibed at all, did so only on festive occasions, and even then with considerable guilt. About a month before Christmas, Mr. McNeil, the railway station master, would keep a sharp eye out for packages of a certain size being unloaded from the Brandon train. When a shoe box sized package wrapped in brown butcher's paper arrived, he would shoot out a hand to the baggage car attendant and say in a low voice to the drayman, "I'll take that, Bill." Bill Conway would nod, and continue stacking cartons of Paulins soda crackers and John Player & Sons cigarettes onto his wagon.

Mr. McNeil would study the address of both recipient and

sender, silently mouthing the words as he read, "Manitoba Liquor Control Board". He then headed into the station house all the while holding the package close to his ample stomach. Gently placing it beside his black candle stick telephone, he would pick up the receiver. "Vi? ... Mr. Bellamy please." Pause.

"Frank, George here," He spoke in a hushed tone of urgency. "Your package has arrived." Long pause.

"OK, you're welcome Frank."

Informing Elwood Elliot that his "package" had arrived was a bit trickier. The school principal's wife, Olive, came from a family of staunch teetotalers. Her mother had been active in the Women's Christian Temperance movement in Toronto before she came to live with her daughter and son in law in Kirkcaldy.

George McNeil always phoned the Elliot residence after school hours to make sure the man of the house was in. "Hello Woody," he would say. "Just wanted to let you know your books are in."

Mr. Elliot had a secret hideaway for his "books" in the basement. It was a small space between the floor joists and a furnace pipe. It was just large enough to accommodate two 26'ers. These he would push into the opening. When they touched the cement foundation, he knew they were completely out of sight.

The Bellamys always dropped by at Christmas to wish the Elliots the best of the season. Mrs. Elliot's announcement that she was off to the kitchen to put on a pot of tea was her husband's cue to say in a rather loud voice, "Frank, while you're here could you give me a hand with that pesky furnace vent?"

"What, stuck again?" Mr. Bellamy would ask in mock surprise.

"'Fraid so," and down the narrow staircase leading into the musty cellar they would go for what Mr. Elliot called, 'a little holiday snort.'

To the northeast of town lay a wooded area everyone called the Big Bush. Large stands of aspen interspersed with birch and scrub oak formed large islands in what would otherwise have been a vast unbroken sea of grass and sage. Through its middle the Assiniboine River wound its unhurried way to Winnipeg to link up with the Red.

It was crown land, and had seen scores of squatters come and go over the years. By the late thirties it was home only to the Metis, better known on the plains as half breeds. White folks seldom ventured into the Big Bush except to cut firewood and pick berries.

In summer hawks circled over its expanses of grass, telescopic eyes trained on the ground below. The slightest stir would bring them spiralling downward, rising with a field mouse or gopher impaled in their talons.

By September their hatchlings were airborne too. Like a meticulously choreographed ballet the young birds caught the wind shooting straight into limitless blue space ... stall, and then drop like a stone only to pull out of the dive to swoop tauntingly into the flight path of a sibling waiting for an updraft. The entire performance was executed at incredible height and speed.

At nightfall the Big Bush sank into the velvet folds of darkness, its silence broken only by the comforting barks of night hunting owls. It still teemed with wild life, but not the way it once had. The black bears were gone and the only reminder of the buffalo was a cabin-sized clump of basalt rock deposited in the middle of an open space by some unknown force eons before. For thousands of years the shaggy beasts had rubbed off their winter wool on its shoulders making it as smooth as an Eskimo carving.

The Metis who lived there were the descendants of Cree mothers and French Canadian and Scottish fur trader fathers. The Prescotts, Fleurys, and Houles kept very much to themselves. Some of their children showed up at school from time to time. Most did not. They lived off the land. Wolf and muskrat traps hung in long rows on the sides of their ramshackle log and mud houses. Skinny dogs of every conceivable color and lineage slinked around the dwellings which were littered with pieces of deer hide and wild animal bones. Some cultivated a small garden at the back of the house.

They rarely came into town, at least not to Kirkcaldy. When they needed staples like sugar, flour or salt, they would hitch their horses to a rickety wagon and head overland to St. Lambert even though it was farther away than Kirkcaldy. The beer parlour in St. Lambert was an attraction, but the Metis seemed to prefer the less judgmental easy going French Canadians over Kirkcaldy's stern Scottish Presbyterian stock.

The Big Bush wasn't left to the Metis out of any sense of benevolence or generosity. Every attempt to exploit it had ended in failure. Daddy Joe Burns, before drink got the better of him, saw oceans of golden wheat rolling over the thousands of acres of open land between the heavy wood growth. It was easy to clear, only buffalo grass and sage to plow under. Joe found himself a partner and took the plunge. Sure enough, the first year the rains came and the wheat grew thick and lush. They took off a bumper crop the likes of which Kirkcaldy had never seen.

Financing was arranged at Ian MacGregor's implement dealership for one of those new fangled harvesting machines called combines. They made a down payment on a Wallace tractor too. Wheat was over a dollar a bushel, and Joe and his partner shipped it out by the carload.

Their bonanza soon evaporated. The light land exhausted itself after the first crop, and yields dropped drastically. The next spring they seeded over a thousand acres and barely got their seed back. The wheat they got went from a dollar a bushel, to eighty-five cents, to twenty-five cents.

It was a sad day indeed for Daddy Joe and his partner when they chugged the still shiny Wallace tractor back to the dealer's with the combine in tow. But he didn't give up. The next year he found himself another partner and started up a saw mill. But there weren't enough big trees to keep it going. He tried sheep, but after the coyotes took their share there weren't enough left to make a living.

Daddy Joe called it quits. He loaded his wife and eight children into his old Model T Ford and left the bush for good. He moved into town, and started making moonshine. The Big Bush was again left to nature and the Metis. One by one they too drifted away. After the last family moved out, the government strung a four strand barbed wire fence around the place and turned it into a community pasture for cattle.

This vast geometry of land and sky was a magical place for a boy. It taught many lessons, like getting to know loneliness; to comprehend and yet not to comprehend the mysteries of rebirth in spring and autumn's gentle reminders of mortality. These were sermons no homily spoken from the pulpit could equal.

But what made Kirkcaldy such a wonderful place for a boy also made it an unfulfilling place for a man. As I matured out of my teens, and even before, I began to long for the social and intellectual intercourse that only an urban environment can offer. I knew I would have to yank up my roots. Not all of them, to be sure. That would have been quite impossible even if I had wanted to.

As a grown man I was drawn back to those roots. I returned to poke around that secure little world of my childhood. I disturbed some ghosts as I knew I would. I also found a dying town. Kirkcaldy had not escaped the blight that to this day afflicts so many prairie towns ... a side effect of progress. There were no sounds of traffic in the streets. Only the wind strumming a mournful tune on the telephone wires.

One farmer with gigantic machines now tills stretches of land that once supported half a dozen families. A paved highway skirts the town providing year-round access to larger centres. The implement dealerships are boarded up. White droppings from generations of sparrows nesting above, decorate the plywood nailed over the windows. A rundown building that looks like Whit Walton's barber shop still stands on Ellice Street. Perhaps it is a barbershop? Probably not, because the farm boys now drive to Brandon to have their hair styled. The brick school is gone. Students are bussed to another one 40 miles away. The roof of the Odd Fellows Hall has collapsed onto the stage below. The railway station is gone too, although the railroad itself has been saved thanks to the potash mine up the line. Bannister's store is still there. It now also serves as the post office. It's a bit shabbier than I remember it.

The grand expectations the old timers once had for Kirkcaldy are long gone. Most of my generation took whatever talent we possessed and went elsewhere. Yet it is this place that is still very much a part of me, and I feel I must honor those who had such high hopes for it. People like Miss Rachel Portman and Franklin Bellamy who never wavered in their efforts to make it a town to be reckoned with. The men broken in body and spirit by God and man made forces over which they had no control like Daddy Joe Burns and Charlie. I must also honor my Mennonite forbears, not necessarily for what they were but for what they strove to be. When World War II broke out in 1939, their principle of pacifism and non-resistance was tested as it had never been tested before. And, in large measure, it was found wanting. Out of 15,000 Canadian Mennonite men of military age, some 6,000 served in the armed forces. Six of those came from Kirkcaldy's small Mennonite community, an enlistment ratio greater than that of the non-Mennonite community.

The war brought about changes. The more thoughtful Mennonites realized that peace is not a natural God-given state, but one that must be constantly re-established...not necessarily by force of arms, but by social and political commitment. The old Mennonite notion that a people can live apart in some kind of utopian agrarian isolation was dashed for all time. Freedom of speech, religion, and physical security through other people's effort and sacrifice became morally indefensible.

Rapid war-time industrialization and massive post war immigration set off an avalanche of urbanization, and Mennonite youth was caught up in its wake. Institutions of higher learning were established, not as cells of isolation to preserve separateness, but to prepare young people to face the challenge of living a Christian life in a world they had no choice but to be a part of. The transition was not easy.

Once you appreciate the validity of life
without a struggle you are equipped with
the basic means of salvation

— Tennessee Williams

BORN AGAIN ... AND AGAIN

I just knew Reverend Heinrich Goertzen was laying for me. I had turned twelve earlier that year, an age when a boy brought up in a Christian, God fearing home, is expected to have developed a finely-tuned sense of right and wrong and a full understanding that his immortal soul stands at the crossroads. One path leading to salvation and life everlasting, the other to damnation and eternal hell fire.

The Rev took it as a direct command from the Almighty Himself to point me in the right direction. It happened the week after the John Deere movies came to Kirkcaldy. Every March the implement company set up a film projector in the Odd Fellows Hall to show farmers the latest line of their machines, and John Deere movie day meant an afternoon off for the school kids. While the farmers came to see the machines, we came for a few yuks when the comic reel came on.

Someone who hadn't come for the laughs was the Reverend Goertzen. He and his slack-jawed son-in-law were there to be entertained only by the hard facts of cultivator weed-kill capability and tractor horsepower in relation to fuel consumption.

The very thought that farm life might have its lighter moments, or that there might be a funny side to the repetitive routine of barnyard chores, was totally contrary to their stern God who demanded nothing less than humorless piety from his highest creation.

For the Rev, the first and last laugh came less than five minutes into the show. Good farmer A is driving past poor farmer B's place on his new tractor ... John Deere of course. Poor farmer B is fixing his dilapidated fence, pounding in a corner post with a rock. Farmer A stops his shiny green Model G, for a chat. B pretends to be unimpressed, lights up his pipe and leans against his newly re-enforced post. The post promptly falls over, sending B and his fence into two feet of brome. Slapstick all the way.

The Reverend didn't even give farmer B a chance to get up and brush himself off. He rose from his seat, straightened himself up to his full five feet four inches, and pointed his ample belly straight for the door. As he passed my seat he gave me one of his Old Testament prophet stares, as if to say you had better leave too.

He didn't look at the Wiens boys sitting in the row in front of me. They were Mennonite too, but being Old Church they were somewhat lower on the redemptive scale. It was the children of the evangelical Brethren, clearly God's chosen, who needed his attention to ensure that the heavenly Brethren circle would be unbroken.

His son-in-law stayed in his seat, engrossed with the drama suddenly unfolding on the screen. Realizing that his soul was in mortal danger in this den of iniquity into which he had so innocently stumbled, he too headed for the door.

I suspected I'd be getting the one-on-one treatment from Goertzen when I failed to go to the front at the previous summer's revival meeting. It had been quite a show, organized by the area's Pentecostal churches with the full support and backing of the Mennonite Brethren.

Weeks before the big event, Jake Friesen had been driving around town and up and down country roads with a huge red and black sign on the roof of his '37 Chevy. On one side were the words ... THE WAGES OF SIN IS DEATH. On the other, FOR GOD SO LOVED THE WORLD THAT HE GAVE HIS ONLY BEGOTTEN SON, THAT WHOSOEVER BELIEVES IN HIM SHALL NOT PERISH BUT HAVE EVERLASTING LIFE."

"Once they've seen that, " Jake used to say, "they've got no excuse."

The "they" although it was never said, were the priest-ridden Catholics, their equally heretical Anglican cousins, the Presbyterians and those worldly Uniteds who condoned smoking and card playing, and whose minister danced.

The spiritual well-being of these benighted, albeit upstanding, citizens whose clergy ran around in black blouses and gave wishy-washy sermons was of minimal concern during the rest of the year.

Brother Ellsworth Carlson, the famed Fargo radio evangelist, was another matter. He was Pentecostal, and when it came to things scriptural there was no pussy-footing around. As Brother Friesen put it, "he sure knows where to lay down the hay so the horses can get at it." No one cheered more enthusiastically than Brother Jake when Ellsworth Carlson was chosen to preach the revival of '42.

Now Jake was a man who took the Bible at its word. There was not a shadow of a doubt in his mind that Lot's wife had turned into a column of salt when she looked back at the condemned town where she'd had such a good time. He took at absolute face value the story of the big fish that swallowed Jonah and spat him out on the beach, and that God had pulled a rib out of Adam to make him a wife.

After burning up all that gas promoting the revival meeting, it was only right that Jake should call for the love offering and introduce Brother Carlson. As a prosperous farmer (he owned the area's largest hog operation and was known as the pig man), the bottom line invariably played a major role in anything he did or said.

"I don't know how many souls Brother Carlson has saved", he told the gathering of townsfolk and leather-faced farmers. "Only God knows that," he intoned as he clutched his dog-eared Bible. "But I do know it's in the thousands. And I also know that for every dollar you give to brother Carlson's ministry you'll get full horsepower in return.

"At this time I'm going to ask the Gospeleers male quartet, with Mrs. Carlson at the piano, to lead us all in the singing of that grand old hymn "Shall We Gather At the River."

The Reverend Mr. Carlson's rich baritone could be heard above all the others.

> *Shall we gather at the river*
> *The beautiful the beautiful river*
> *Gather with the saints at the river*
> *That flows by the throne of God*

Carlson was a large man in his late 30's with thick blond hair. He was shod in white shoes, his broad shoulders molded into a well-fitting tan gabardine suit. He was younger than I had imagined listening to him on the radio. The posters announcing his coming proclaimed that in his youth he'd been a boxer of some renown, and had played full-back on a college football team in Georgia.

He told the assembly how thankful he was that the Lord had brought him to Kirkcaldy to meet, in person, the folks who had

27

been so generous in supporting his radio ministry. "As long as you folks keep on givin', I'll keep on tellin' the greatest story ever written — the story of Jesus and his love. Let's all stand and sing that wonderful song *I Love to Tell the Story.*"

Carlson's powerful voice again soared high above the crowd...up, up into the blue July sky. Even before the last strains had faded away Carlson bowed his head. There was a long pause. In later years I would wonder whether it was a quiet prayer seeking divine inspiration, or done for dramatic effect. He slowly raised his head. "The text I have chose is from Luke...Luke 13," his voice boomed out like a church organ.

It was the story of Christ teaching in the villages. Someone asks Him, "Lord, are there just a few who are being saved?"

With that question Carlson launched into his message, playing the crowd like a finely-tuned fiddle. One moment his voice was strong and authoritative, the next quivering and weepy as he talked about all the sinners who would be knocking on the door of salvation after the Lord had closed it for all time. Closed to all those who would not heed his call. And yes, Jesus was speaking this very hour to the sinners of Kirkcaldy gathered on this school ground under these rustling cottonwoods. Would the door still be open tomorrow or, he sobbed, "will this be the night your soul will be required of you?"

Would Jesus stand behind that closed door, and with a broken heart listen to your weeping and gnashing of teeth on the other side? Would you be locked out forever?

A scattering of sniffles broke out. Women reached into their purses for stiffly starched white hankies. One young girl, perhaps fourteen, began sobbing uncontrollably. A large shouldered woman in a flowered dress pulled the girl to her bosom and began to gently stroke her hair.

Carlson started praying. He said he knew the Lord was speaking to many in the crowd and invited the lost to come forward. As his prayer came to a close, Mrs. Carlson began playing the piano ever so softly, and the Gospeleers sang.

Almost persuaded, now to believe
Almost persuaded Christ to receive
Seems now some soul to say,
Go Saviour, go thy way
Some more convenient day
On thee I'll call.

The quartet segued to a hum as Carlson spoke, "If you are lost, the door stands open for you today. Come forward. Let us pray for you and with you. You know who you are and Jesus knows who you are. Do not wait until the door is closed forever. Come. Come through the open door of salvation."

The sobbing girl was first to go. She was followed by a middle aged man with a purplish nose and a slightly wobbly gait. He was the same man I'd seen go to the front at last summer's revival. Then, my older cousin Ike, moving like a sleepwalker, went forward.

Face turned heavenward, Carlson led the quartet and the assemblage into the final hymn but first reciting the words -

> *Just as I am without one plea*
> *But that thy blood was shed for me.......*
> *I come. I come.*

I caught my mother's pleading glance from the other side of the dirt aisle. Her wordless message was unmistakable, "Won't you go forward too? Please?"

Salty tears welled in my eyes and I began wiping them away with the back of my hand. "I could go forward," I said to myself, "but what do I do when I get there? I certainly don't want to disappoint Jesus. But what should I say to him?"

My feet felt like blocks of lead weighing me down. With the best will in the world I couldn't move. Was I saying to the saviour, "on some more convenient day on thee I'll call?"

I didn't call, but the Reverend Heinrich Goertzen did...that next winter.

"But...I can't. I've got to check my trapline before it gets dark," I pleaded with my mother who had intercepted me on the way to my room after school." "Not today," she said firmly. "Mr. Goertzen has something to say to you."

The Reverend sat in the living room with my father. He gave me a tight smile. "You must put important things first," he admonished, having overhead the conversation with my mother. "Things of this world can wait. Your soul and where you spend eternity is all that really matters, don't you think?"

I didn't answer. The only eternity that had preoccupied me that day was watching the big wall clock in Room 3 agonizingly tick its way toward four. And when a sixth grade boy has to choose between eternal life and the school's out bell, eternal life doesn't stand a chance.

"How old are you now?" Goertzen asked. He knew very well how old I was.

"Twelve."

"Do you pray every night?"

"Yes."

"And what do you pray? What do you say to Jesus?"

It was an embarrassing question. Here I was twelve years old and still reciting the same little child's prayer my mother had taught me when I was five. In German.

Lieber Heiland
Mach mich fromm
Das Ich in dem Himmel komm.
(Dear Lord, Make me good
So I'll go to heaven)

"That's very nice. But aren't you a little old for that kind of a prayer?" I admitted that I probably was, but secretly felt that it wasn't too bad a prayer. It seemed to cover all the essentials with a minimum of words.

"Do you sometimes do bad things?"

"Yes."

"And what kind of bad things do you do?"

"Well, sometimes I don't do my chores when I'm supposed to. Sometimes I get into fights at school."

"You realize, don't you, that when you do things like that and, by the way, laugh at funny films your teachers let you watch, you are sinning?" I remained silent.

Goertzen cleared his throat, looked somewhat nervously at my mother, and suggested I might at times have improper thoughts. Perhaps commit secret sins which he assumed every young boy indulged in. He quickly shifted to more comfortable theological ground.

"Even if we were all perfect," he purred, "we would still be in need of God's forgiveness. You see, all of us have inherited sin from the very first sinners...Adam and Eve."

Although Goertzen had me blubbering in my cupped hands, this declaration of infallible doctrine which I'd heard so often in

Sunday school, fanned a dormant spark of rebellion. Why I should have to carry the can for two adults who had everything going for them, and were stupid enough to let a snake talk them into eating forbidden fruit, was totally incomprehensible to me.

"Would you like to kneel with me and your parents and ask Jesus to come into your heart? If you do that, He will wash it clean with the blood He shed for you on the cross."

I nodded my head. Goertzen prayed first. He thanked the Lord for his personal salvation. It was a story I, and everyone in our church, knew well because he told it in practically every sermon he preached.

As a young man in Russia, he'd been the world's biggest hypocrite pretending to be a Christian, all the while living a sinful life. While travelling by sled across the Siberian steppes, taking his parents and a visiting preacher to a neighboring Mennonite village, he'd come face to face with God much like Paul had done on the road to Damascus.

A blizzard was brewing, so the young Goertzen bent over to pick up the whip to hurry on his tired team of horses. To his horror his tobacco pouch fell out of his pocket. In a flash (in some versions of the story he told of seeing a light), he grabbed the pouch and hurled it as far as he could. Then and there he knelt in the swirling snow with his parents and the preacher and gave himself to Christ.

Nothing remotely as dramatic was taking place in the old farm house at Kirkcaldy on that winter's day. When it was my turn to pray...to open my heart to the same God who had saved the Reverend Goertzen in the snows of Siberia, my tongue felt as though it was glued to the roof of my mouth. The whole room was swimming through my tears.

There was a long, awkward silence. Realizing that I wasn't about to utter a word, Goertzen asked me to follow him in prayer.

"Dear Lord, I ask you to forgive my sins and come into my heart." I repeated the words. Again dead silence. Realizing that he had failed to prime the outpouring of guilt and repentance he had hoped for, he continued; "I am unworthy of salvation." Again I repeated.

"It is the precious blood of your Son."
"It is the precious blood of your Son."
"Who died on the cross for my sins."
"Who died on the cross for my sins."
"And whom I accept in my heart today."
"And whom I accept in my heart today."
"Amen."
"Amen."

We all arose. Goertzen gave me a look that had skepticism written all over it. My mother had the same puzzled look I'd seen on her face when the centre of a promising cake fell while it was baking in the oven. My father glanced nervously at his pocket watch and allowed as how the hour was getting late he'd better get the milking started.

As for me, no heavy load had rolled off my shoulders as had happened to some of the people I'd heard testify in church. Or maybe, like Jake Friesen said in one of his testimonials, "if you carry that load around on your back long enough you get so used to it you don't even know it's there." Come to think of it, that Jake was pretty good at putting the hay down where the horses could get at it himself.

That night on my way to bed, I overheard my parents discussing my 'conversion'.

"Maybe he's still too young to understand", my mother said.

"Well", my father replied, "Toews from Winnipeg will be here for next summer's revival meeting. We'll give it another try then."

Let us dig into the past where old friends
and enemies lie buried and preserved
— Seamus Heaney

BE A GOODA BOY

Ol' Rock used to say that old folks always die in spring or just before the snow flies. They either lose the will to face another prairie winter or, if they've made it to spring break up, they expire from the exhaustion of the effort. "Guess Ol' Rock couldn't face another winter," I thought as I saw him lying on his bed, if you could call it a bed. As I recall it was nothing more than a collection of wooden crates stacked one over the other. A tattered mattress rested on top.

Ol' Rock lay under a frayed sheet which was covered by a well-worn horse blanket with straps and buckles cut off. Both his stockinged feet stuck out over the end of the bed. One big toe, its nail gnarled and yellow, had worked its way through a thick woolen sock. His heavy mustache, which should have been white like the silver mound of hair on his head, was yellow too. It had a brown blotch in one corner where his curled pipe had rested during his every waking hour.

His muscular frame belied his 70 years. A large hand at the end of a hair-matted arm, the thickness of a horse's leg, protruded from under the covers. Its size was mute testimony to the countless pieces of glowing steel it had pounded into the desired shape.

Only minutes before I had threaded my way through his cluttered blacksmith shop - past the huge forge that stood cold and menacing, like some malevolent ruler surveying a dark and dank domain; past the massive anvil, the rack of long and short tongs, the deflated bellows and a scattering of hammers of every conceivable shape and size. The water in the concrete cooling tub, which hissed and belched like an enraged dragon, when red hot metal was thrust into it, was a solid block of black ice.

Ol' Rock's shop, and his cramped living quarters at the back, were as familiar to me as our own farm house. I visited him often, usually after school broke for the noon hour. The town kids went home for lunch, the older farm boys wolfed down their baloney sandwiches and rushed off to Gene Gauthier's Cafe and Billiards for a game of Boston.

As a Mennonite I was warned never to darken the doorway of a pool hall or, heaven forbid, a movie theatre or dance hall. I wasn't supposed to frequent Ol' Rock's place either. Not that he was a bad person, but my parents would not have understood a friendship between an old man and a 14 year old boy. Besides, he was a Catholic.

He had a small crucifix that hung at a slight angle over his bed. It was a tiny Christ nailed to a miniature cross. Trickles of blood ran across its face from a crown of thorns and from a red pin prick on its right side.

"That's the problem with Catholics," my father would say, "they've never taken Christ down from the cross. We Mennonites, on the other hand, worship the true, living risen Christ."

Ol' Rock never talked religion. The closest he came to mentioning the subject was one day when he was catching a ride to St. Lambert with Bob Lowes' transfer truck. He had asked me to clear some metal scraps out of the shop while he was gone.

I goa Santa Lambert today. Seea padre. Getta cleaned out inside." he said, placing one hand over his heart. "I paya you a quarter tomorrow. Now be a gooda boy."

He always said that whenever we took our leave. He never said 'good bye' or 'so long', it was always "now be a gooda boy."

And when he said he'd pay me the next day for doing a job, he always did. I didn't get paid for doing chores around the farm and didn't expect it. My father, however, did invariably promise to give me a dollar for doing man's work at harvest time, and just as invariably it would slip his mind.

Ol' Rock's place was a sanctuary, a respite from a home where there was too much discipline and too little love. It was a perfect place to slide into a sagging easy chair in front of the Good Morning heater with a back copy of *National Geographic*. The ones about Africa interested me most. And whenever Ol' Rock caught me skipping past the lions and zebras to peek at the lithe brown-skinned topless girls, he would peer over his wire-rimmed glasses, mockingly shake his finger and say, "now, be a gooda boy."

Another attraction was his wind-up gramophone. With the deft touch of a surgeon's hand he would slip a 78 disc out of its sleeve and gently drop it onto the turntable. After a few seconds of rhythmic scraping Enrico Caruso's slightly metallic voice, singing an aria from Puccini or Verdi, would soar from the tiny speaker. Each aria told a story, and Ol' Rock knew them all. "That'sa Cavarodossi," he would whisper. "He gonna be killed. He sing gooda bye to his lovely Tosca." Ol' Rock claimed that when he heard Caruso sing on stage in Chicago once, he had actually felt the warm sun of Italy on his face.

My parents wouldn't allow a phonograph in the house; a devil's instrument, my father called it. But I did own one Wilf Carter recording. On one side was *The Strawberry Roan*, and on the other, of lesser importance, *When It's Springtime in the Rockies*.

I kept my secret possession at Ol Rock's place. He would remove his pipe, blow away any dust or lint that might have lodged in its grooves and put it on the machine for me. Having done so he would suddenly think of some task that needed immediate doing leaving me alone with Wilf and that untamable steed, the Strawberry Roan.

How I got that record is another story. It could almost be said that it was the Lord's will. Well, it may not have exactly been His will, but if Blanche Pentland hadn't gotten herself saved by one of those American evangelists on the Fargo radio station, I'd never have owned that record.

As a born again Christian Miss Pentland, a spinster and retired school teacher, thought it best to ditch her worldly record collection. I came across the pile of smashed discs at the town dump, her name still neatly printed on the jackets. There were fox trots, waltzes, a few marches and a disc of *Humoresque*, and *The Whistler and his Dog*. Then there were the Wilf Carter numbers; the stories of Pete Knight, the cowboy's cowboy, and Albert Johnson, the Mad Trapper. Only the Strawberry Roan had miraculously survived.

There were also books with titles like, *A Stormy Life, Wayward Feet* and *Marked for Life*. I didn't pick them up. I felt I was already pushing my luck with the 'roan'.

I knew Ol' Rock was dead the moment I laid eyes on him. His face was the colour of the ashes on the floor in front of the cast-iron heater. His mouth was partly open revealing rows of brown teeth.

I also knew I'd have to tell Franklin Bellamy right away. Mr. Bellamy was the municipal secretary and handled everything of consequence in Kirkcaldy - and this was certainly an important matter.

"And what business brought you to Mr. Rocola's blacksmith shop young man?" Mr. Bellamy asked, looking not at me, to whom the question had obviously been directed, but at John Lawson. Mr. Bellamy had phoned him as soon as he got the news.

Mr. Lawson operated the Red & White grocery store, the butcher shop and the town's funeral parlour. In winter sides of beef hung in the front of a long shed behind his store. The undertaker part was behind a partition at the back.

Mr. Bellamy glanced my way still waiting for an answer. "I came to listen to some records on his gramophone. I do that lots of times during the lunch hour."

Mr. Bellamy said nothing. He walked over to the side of the bed where Mr. Lawson had pulled back the covers. Ol' Rock had gone to bed in his long johns, which I suspected he always did when it got cold.

"No marks that I can see," Mr. Lawson said, looking up at Mr. Bellamy. "I think the old ticker just conked out, Frank."

"When was the last time you saw Mr. Rocola young fella?" Mr. Bellamy asked.

"Yesterday," I said. "And he was feeling good, as far as I could tell."

"Well, you'd better run along now."

I was turning to leave when Mr. Lawson shouted, "Wait a minute. Ever see Mr. Rocola hide anything? I mean stash something someplace out of sight?"

"Nope. Never did."

I hadn't been entirely truthful. Ol' Rock did keep a large cigar box in a space between the sloping plank roof and the north wall. If the wall and ceiling had met flush the way they were supposed to the opening wouldn't have existed. But as it was, there was a crevice just large enough to conceal the box. I knew the box was there, but I'd managed to resist the temptation to look inside. I figured that if Ol' Rock wanted me to see what was in there he wouldn't have put it away. Technically, I hadn't lied to Mr. Lawson because I'd never actually seen him hide the box.

Even if I had lied, I wasn't sorry. Mr. Lawson was the last person I wanted to see get his hands on anything that belonged to Ol' Rock. The joke around town was that anyone who shook hands with Lawson had better count their fingers when they got their hand back. My father, who always counted his change very carefully, counted it twice when he bought anything at the Lawson store.

I doubted that Mr. Lawson would have had the slightest interest in Ol' Rock if it hadn't been for the rumours. Gossip had it that he had a pile of money hidden away somewhere in his cluttered shop.

The money came from his sons who, it was rumoured, were gangsters in the States. It was true that Ol' Rock had come to Kirkcaldy from the United States in the late 20's and that he had two sons.

An enlarged family photo was tacked on the wall opposite the crucifix. He had told me the picture was taken in the old country and that his wife, dressed entirely in black except for a white embroidered collar on her dress, had died soon after they had arrived in America. There were four young girls in the picture and two boys, all standing behind their parents who were seated on chairs. Ol' Rock was sitting ram-rod straight, his huge hands draped over his knees. His mustache and hair were jet black.

I was most interested in the boys who appeared to be in their early teens. Like the rest of the family there wasn't so much as the suggestion of a smile on their faces. The younger boy was called Antonio. The oldest boy was Giuseppe. Rock had named him after Verdi, his favourite composer.

I was pretty sure that Mr. Lawson didn't know or care anything about opera, but he could, as his best friend Mr. Bellamy once said, "hear a dollar bill drop". And money is what he smelled in the stale, soot-filled blacksmith shop.

"The old coot got another cheque from the States just last week. A thousand bucks," Flo Parker half whispered to Mr. Lawson as she poured him a second cup of coffee. Flo worked behind the counter at Gauthier's Cafe afternoons, and in the mornings she sorted mail for her arthritic mother who ran the post office.

Mr. Lawson gave a low whistle. "A thousand bucks. Half the people around here don't make that in a year."

"That's a thousand American, John."

Flo picked up a bottle of ketchup and proceeded to wipe off

imaginary stains. "Yep, been getting one of those every six months or so. Seen 'em myself." She caught herself, and abruptly stopped speaking, nervously scanning the tables to see if she'd been overheard. From where I was sitting I could distinctly hear the conversation over the click of the billiard balls behind the poolroom door.

Since Ol' Rock died, I'd been spending more time at the Cafe waiting for the other boys to finish playing pool. I pretended to be immersed in a Dick Tracy comic book I was reading for the third time, and turned a page with a look of exaggerated concentration.

Flo picked up the salt and pepper and swished a cloth over the counter top.

"No business in town will touch cheques that size," Mr. Lawson said, "Where does he cash 'em?"

"The bank in St. Lambert. Why'd'ya think he was always catching a ride with Bobby on his truck run?"

"Brings the cash back and stuffs it into his mattress I guess", Mr. Lawson said with a tight laugh.

"So, when ya gonna deep six him?" Flo asked.

"Don't know. Depends on when somebody shows up to pay the bills."

"Guess there's no big rush", Flo said.

"Nope, she was 20 below again last night. No snow, so the ground's hard as a stone and the old geezer's froze stiff as a board." Mr. Lawson stirred some more sugar into his coffee before speaking.

"Frank phoned Father LaPierre in St. Lambert. Figures the father might know how to contact the family and arrange a Catholic burial."

The day after they loaded Ol' Rock onto Bob Lowes' three ton and hauled him off to St. Lambert, I took the long way around past his shop on my way to the Cafe. I always went that way after he died. I imagined seeing him trying to pull a piece of metal from the tangled pile of scrap beside his shop like he used to do.

"Hello, Mr. Rocola," I'd yell in my silly imaginary game, "I'll give you a hand." With a mighty yank we'd pull the piece of metal free. He would smile and say, "Hey, you a gooda boy."

I knew of course that when I got to the scrap pile he wouldn't be there. But on this particular day someone else was. Parked beside the shop was the longest, shiniest chrome-trimmed car I had ever seen. She was, what the magazine ads of the day called, "streamlined." When I looked at the licence plate, I knew it was foreign. Besides the number there was printing on it - "ILL-IN-OIS. LAND OF LINCOLN." On the trunk in fancy chrome scroll was the car's make - La Salle.

"Want sump'in kid?"

"No, No," I stammered in response to the short, swarthy man who had quietly come up behind me. "Just looking at your car."

"Well, you looked. Now scram."

I was about to go on my way when another man appeared from the side of the shop. He looked like he'd beat you up if he didn't like the way you parted your hair.

"Beats me if I know how to get into the place Joe," he said.

"Hell, just rip the bloody door off." Joe replied.

"You want to get into Ol' R—I mean, Mr. Rocola's place?" I asked.

"Yeh", said Joe. "you know who's got the key?"

"There's no key", I said, reaching for the spike lying on a window ledge. I pushed it through the small opening Ol' Rock had whittled through the door, and flipped up the wooden latch on the inside.

"Looks like you been here before", Joe said.

"Yeh, used to come here lots. Ol' R—I mean, Mr. Rocola, played records for me. Let me read his magazines".

By now, I knew the two men were the boys I'd seen in the picture.

"You've got to walk through here to get to his room," I said with an air of self-importance.

We edged our way past the forge heaped high with charcoal and past the soot-caked cooling tub. Both men took great care not to smudge their finely tailored coats and glossy black shoes. I had never seen such snappy dressers. The male models in Eaton's catalogue and even Mr. Bellamy who was considered a bit of a dandy around town, simply weren't in the same league.

The door to Ol' Rock's room was open. Nothing appeared to be out of place, except the mattress was gone. Joe opened a cardboard box sitting beside the bed and shook it gently. Some crudely darned socks and a pair of long fleece-lined underwear tumbled out. He then took the crucifix and family photo off the wall and stuffed them into his coat pocket.

It was then that I remembered the cigar box. "Do you want his cigar box", I asked.

"Cigar box? What cigar box?" Joe asked.

"It's up here," I said, reaching into the cubby hole above the wall.

Joe spilled its contents onto a small wooden table beside the heater. Two large copper pennies, the kind they weren't making anymore, rolled onto the floor. The rest of the stuff made a neat pile on the table - a string of beads with a small metal cross attached, a woman's brooch trimmed with silver filagree and three small photos, cracked and yellowing around the edges. There were also about half a dozen envelopes, with what appeared to be Ol' Rock's address on them, bearing American stamps and a somewhat smaller envelope with a Canadian stamp.

Joe picked up the Canadian letter and removed a typewritten note. "Hey Tony, that priest in St. Lambert says thanks here to the old man for helping out some damn home for delinquent boys." He handed the note to his brother. Tony's lips moved as he read, but he said nothing. When he was finished he rolled the note up into a tight ball and dropped it into the heater.

He scooped up the rosary and the brooch and pushed them into his coat pocket. As he did so, the light caught the ring on his pinky setting off an explosion of pale blue flashes the likes of which I had never seen.

Silently, both men walked back to their car. Joe slipped the gear shift into low with one hand and rolled down the window with the other.

"Thanks", he said, handing me a five dollar bill.."And hey, kid" he added almost as an afterthought - "You be a good boy - ya hear?"

I watched the La Salle round the corner at Lawson's Red & White, point its long sleek nose due South toward the American border and disappear.

It was then that I noticed large snowflakes floating down from the grey sky. It was the first snow of the winter. Ol' Rock used to say that whenever it starts snowing, it's sure to warm up. And it always did.

There passed a weary time, each throat
was parched, and glazed each eye
A weary time! A weary time!
— S. T. Coleridge

DROUGHT

It hadn't rained for more than two months. The countryside lay lethargic and exhausted. An unrelenting hot wind blew in from the southeast, and night failed to bring the usual relief. The earth hardened and cracked. The soil felt hot to the touch and the grass turned a rusty red. Blades that managed to suck meagre sustenance from a ditch or hollow were shorn to ground level by swarms of grasshoppers.

Seeded crops, which had sprouted with such promise, wilted to a pale green, then died. The tilled soil drifted like black snow against buildings and fences, burying posts. It came in through the shrunken window frames settling on sills. It choked its way into the caragana hedges and lilac bushes.

Cattle stood bawling knee deep in slough mud, waiting to be watered. The well pump coaxed a slow trickle to the surface for a few minutes if enough ground water was allowed to gather between pumpings.

Animals and birds, normally wary of humans, became tame, as if looking to God's higher creation for relief from thirst. A half-crazed ground hog ambled across the farm yard in search of water. The dogs watched him from their lair under the kitchen porch, but didn't move.

For all the dryness, the fields shimmered and rippled under what appeared to be a sea of blue water - a mirage created by the sun's rays striking different atmospheric densities.

There was a hush in every farm kitchen when the weather forecast came on over the radio. It often gave faint promises of "systems" moving in from the Pacific, but they never materialized, or if they did they never amounted to anything. Soon the reports were either ignored, or not listened to at all. At church, prayers for rain become less frequent, as though the leather-faced farmers were thinking that Matthew might just as easily have said that God does not send rain on the righteous and the unrighteous.

A few times the sky turned black as India ink. A sprinkling of mocking drops pockmarked the dust, then the clouds cleared leaving the earth once again at the mercy of the sun's glare.

For all we knew, it might never rain again. The prairie heat that had always spawned drenching thunderstorms was impotent. The rain-bearing south westerlies refused to blow. Had all the laws of science been changed? Found to be invalid?

One night there was a flicker of light on my bedroom wall. Then another. The third illuminated the roses on the wallpaper. I couldn't stay in bed. I leapt up and ran outside in my bare feet. For once the flagstoned walk felt cool. The air was deathly still. Nothing stirred.

Banks of sheet lightning lit up clouds resting on the rim of the western horizon. Every few seconds, like a distant artillery barrage, there was the low rumble of rolling thunder. I went back to bed. For the first time that summer I had confidence in my hopes. I lay still, not moving a muscle. Then I heard it - a distinct splat on the roof. Another on the window pane. The staccato turned into a roaring crescendo of cascading water. I listened to that sweet sound for nearly two hours. It was still raining when I fell asleep. But outside all creation was wide awake. Drinking. Drinking deeply. The drought was over.

Oh I have slipped the surly bonds of
earth, And danced the skies on
laughter ~ silvered wings

— John Gillespie Magee

THE YELLOW PERILS

I had the landing strip all picked out. The north quarter. Flat as a pool table, no rocks and wide enough to let a plane come in from any direction. The perfect place to put down a Tiger Moth.

The skies were dotted with these yellow biplanes when the weather was clear, and on the prairies that's pretty well every day.

The boys flying the Moths, and a variety of other craft, were Brits, Canadians, Australians, New Zealanders and about six thousand Americans serving in the RCAF. (The United States still wasn't in World War II). They were forever becoming disoriented by the limitless space above them, and the equally vast and featureless expanse of land below. They would try to find their bearings by following the main CPR line back to their base at Warden. They called the railway the "steel compass." Often they were sidetracked by a meandering branchline only to find themselves at the far end of nowhere buzzing grain elevators trying to read the town's name and find it on a road map they carried in the cockpit.

One eighteen year old complained that every town was named Ogilvie until it was explained to him that the elevators belonged to the Ogilvie grain company.

One sunny fall day, a spotty-faced boy from Birmingham, England circled the elevators, read Kirkcaldy and couldn't find it on his map. He was out of gas anyway so he landed on a farmer's field next to the school's baseball diamond. He was a good four miles shy of the field I'd picked out for just such an emergency landing.

Miss Rachel Portman, never one to miss an opportunity for her students to learn, put the bewildered lad in front of the blackboard, and instructed him to give a talk on the British Isles while he waited for the fuel truck to arrive from the base.

My dream of having an honest-to-goodness airforce plane land on our farm nearly came true. (But then, as one of our English neighbours was fond of saying, nearly never killed a man). And it would have come true if my father hadn't been so particular about getting his fall plowing done.

It was winter. A Saturday. The sunflower yellow Tiger Moth circled slowly over the north quarter. The pilot, wearing a helmet and goggles, was clearly visible. 'Student flying solo. Running out of gas.' I thought to myself as I heard two distinct coughs coming from the engine. My heart thumped as he swooped low over my designated landing field and then, to my horror, he kept right on going over the fence into the next field, and the next, disappearing somewhere over the McNaughton farm.

"Rats, he's landing at Jimmy McNaughton's place," I muttered under my breath. Now Jimmy would be bragging all over school that an airforce plane had landed on their farm. And he didn't even know anything about planes. Why he wouldn't know a Tiger Moth from a Gypsy Moth, Fairey Battle or Hurricane.

When I got to the McNaughton farm the shivering but unhurt pilot was sitting beside the kitchen stove still in his leather bomber jacket and massive fleece-lined flight boots. His plane was parked in a stubble field behind the barn.

"I was preparing to put down a mile east," he said with a somewhat lilting accent, "but I saw black clods poking up out of the snow. A plowed field isn't the best place to land with skis."

My heart sank. Of course. In winter they're on skis. They don't like landing on plowed fields.

"So," the pilot went on, "I was just flying on petrol fumes when I saw your nice stubble field. She came in smooth as silk."

"And wherre arre ye frrom?" Mrs. McNaughton asked, as she poured him a cup of hot cocoa. She was Scotch, and when she spoke, her r's vibrated making a sound like a piece of stiff cardboard rubbing against bike spokes at full speed.

"From Wales. Little place called Welwyn."

"Well, Lorrd, love a duck laddie. Welwyn, Wales," she trilled. "If you'd have gone anotherr fourr miles down the line you'd have landed in Welwyn, Saskatchewan."

I had to reluctantly concede that the McNaughton farm had been a better place to land. It wasn't just the plowed field. The McNaughtons had a phone to call the base at Warden, but most importantly, they were the pilot's own kind. While my parents had no liking for the Nazis, they would have felt awkward accommodating an "English" person, especially one who was training to rain bombs on innocent children and old people.

This antipathy towards anything having to do with the war didn't dampen my secret preoccupation with it, and with the airforce in particular. How could any red-blooded young boy not be? It was a rare day when there wasn't a "yellow peril," as the locals called the airforce planes, or a formation of them, roaring across the electric blue prairie skies.

This passion for flight was shared by my best friend, John Hiebert, who lived near Brandon. It was the main subject of our correspondence.

April 30th, 1941
Norman, Man.

Dear Abe,

How are you? I am fine. The snow is gone and we are playing baseball already at school and drowning gofers but what I am really riting about is the harvard crash and Dennis Chambers steeling the pilots ristwach. It crasht yesterday on that big hill on Dunsmore's farm near the school. It came down so low the windows in the school rattled real hard. I knew right away it was a harvard because the sound it made theyr real high powered. The plane was smasht up real bad but there was no fire and it didnt explode. I figgered the pilot switcht off the gas just before he crasht and killed hiself. Me and Dennis could see him in the cockpit his arm kind of sticking out the side.

He had a ristwach on and I know Dennis stole it. He says I am lying but I know Dennis stole it. He says I am lying but I know hes got it. Dennis is real dum in grad 5 he is 15 and will be old enuf to quit school soon. I want to stay in school. Minninites arent supposed to but I sure want to be a pilot somday and they need to be good in aritmitic. The airforce and police came out from Brandon to get the pilot they are suppose to move the reck tomorrow. Mr. Dunsmore told our teacher one of his girls Lorna was going out with the pilot who was an American in the RCAF and that he was flying low over there

farm to show off when he crasht. Please rite back soon.
your friend,
John.

June 15th, 1941

Dear John,
How are things with you? Everything here is fine. We have two
more weeks of school I'll sure be glad when summer holidays
come even if it means more work around the farm. Sure lots of
excitement at your school and we had some too. A Fairey Battle
it was not paynted yellow it was paynted comoflage came in real
low over school last friday on our last recess. It made two passes and the second time was so low I seen exaust coming out the
pipes on the side. The pilot threw a small canister out of the
cockpit it was like a cardbord tin can and white and it landed
in left field. Doug Burns from my grade picked it up and gave
it to Miss Portman and she opened it and there was a note
inside it said hello Miss Portman, your formr student Bud
Anderson. She said he went to our school once. I will end for
now. Dad wants me to start milking.
Write soon.
your friend,
Abe

June 22nd, 1941,

Dear Abe,
   How are you? I am fine. summer holidays will soon be here
and it is sure hard to sit in school when it is so nice out. The
place where the harvard crast is cleened up now exept for the
oil on the ground. The police were at school looking for the ristwach Dennis stole offen the pilot. He said he didint take it but
I knew he was lying because I knew he kept it in his overalls
pocket. The mountie who came to school told us they had sent
all the pilots stuff back to the states and his parents wanted to
know what happned to his ristwach with his name ingraved on
the back because it was a graduashin present. The mountie
asked me if I knew anything about it and I said no because I
didnt want Dennis to beet me up if I told on him. We came in

49

from last recess and the mountie was still sitting in his car. When we came in the clock by the blackboard was stoppt. None of us kids owns a wach but recess is haf past two and when we came back it was still haf past two. Dennis is pretty dum but he knew the clock was wrong because he waches it all the time. I saw him pull the ristwach from his pocket and try to hide it. I gess the teacher saw it to because she asked Dennis what he had and he said nothing. She called the mountie and dismist everybody exept Dennis and took the ristwach offen him. Dennis wont be old enuf to quit school til october but the teacher said he didnt have to come back no more.

Rite soon. Your friend,

John.

So while I, and thousands of other Canadian boys my age, were counting the days to our eighteenth birthday so we could 'join up' my parents prayed fervently that the war would soon end.

Just how I would overcome my parents' and the church's strenuous opposition to such a reckless, not to mention sinful, act as serving in the military I had not yet resolved. My friend John, who was a bit of a joker, said we'd jump off that bridge when we got to it. As it turned out we never got to the bridge. A month after I filled out my draft registration Germany surrendered. My friends were quick to assure me that the two events were in no way connected.

Oh the quest of our patrol
Is a question rather droll...

— lyrics from Jungle Book

Richard and Robert Sherman

THE GERMANS ARE COMING
.... THE GERMANS ARE COMING

DO YOUR BIT, proclaimed the hand-lettered poster. THE EMPIRE STANDS IN PERIL. JOIN THE KIRKCALDY HOME GUARD. It informed all and sundry that Kirkcaldy was mobilizing. Issued under the authority of John Pearkes (Sgt. Retired) it called all able bodied men to attend a meeting at the Odd Fellows Hall, at which time a home guard unit would be organized.

These were the dark days of the summer of 1940. Hitler's blitzkrieg had crushed the Lowlands, swept across France at lightning speed, and pushed the French and British troops onto a spit of sand on the Channel near Dunkirk. The Fuehrer stood astride Europe, poised to thrust a dagger into the very heart of Mother England herself.

Kirkcaldyites were thinking the unthinkable. Hob-nailed German jack boots tramping through the hallowed halls of Westminster Abbey, St. Paul's, The Houses of Parliament, and, horror of horrors, the royal household itself, Buckingham Palace. And then, would it only be a matter of time before Canada, the brightest jewel in the crown of the British Empire would suffer the same fate? Nazi U-boats were already snooping around the Gulf of St. Lawrence.

"We can't expect any help from the Americans", the parade square voice of Sergeant Pearkes boomed out to the gathering of mostly World War I veterans. "They had to be dragged kicking and screaming into the last war, and then tried to take all the credit for defeating the Hun. Now, they're sitting on their duffs again."

He explained that if the Nazi juggernaut had to be met head on in Canada, perhaps on the prairies, maybe even in Kirkcaldy, he was sure there wasn't a man in the community who wouldn't stand up and fight.

Pearkes decreed that the Kirkcaldy Home Guard would rendezvous behind the lumber yard Wednesday and Saturday evenings. There was no money for uniforms of any kind so, he said, anyone who could lay their hands on World War I surplus kit like tin hats, tunics, caps or web belts, should wear same on parade.

A committee was struck to organize a burning of Hitler in effigy. (The burning of the Kaiser's likeness twenty-five years earlier had been a huge success.) Someone was nominated to contact the Ladies' Aid to see if refreshments could be arranged for the event.

A suggestion that rifle practice be part of the training was voted down because of the ammunition shortage. One of the few farmers present implored anyone who could spare a few rounds to hone their marksmanship on an explosion of gophers in his cow pasture.

"If we're not going to fire rifles", one of them griped, "what are we going to do?"

"March", bellowed Pearkes, "We're bloody well going to march and we're going to drill."

And march they did. Hup, two, three, four. Hup, two, three, four. Down the road behind the lumber yard, past the pile of scrap iron back of Old Rock's blacksmith shop, through the main gate of the sports ground, then a sharp turn to the right. From there the newly formed unit proceeded double file around the perimeter of the field. Wellington Legget-Bourke (everybody called him Duke) was odd man out and brought up the rear single file. His feet were giving him trouble, tripping over sods tossed near the fence when the pitcher's mound was enlarged.

"Get into step," Pearkes roared at Big Bob Murdoch. "I am in step", Big Bob shot back, "it's all these other buggers that ain't."

The body of men was thrown off stride when they tried to maneuver a dog leg in front of the shuttered hamburger and lemonade stands near the exit gate. Big Bob did a quick little dance to get back in step, but seeing that the others weren't even trying, he gave up too.

When the two wobbly lines of wheezing men got back to the lumber yard, Pearkes had them form a single line. He rolled his eyes heavenward ever so briefly, then barked, "Company dismissed."

The men eased themselves onto piles of stacked lumber. Some pulled tobacco pouches from back pockets and rolled cigarettes. Others took out pipes carried in the bibs of blue overalls inside which they had lived for the better part of their lives.

53

As if by magic, several cases of beer appeared. Soon some-body started blowing on a mouth organ, and Duke was leading a lusty sing along of Great War songs...*Pack Up Your Troubles* and *Mademoiselle From Armentieres.*

"Legs" McCreary and I had viewed the march from the sports ground gate, and now watched the company unwind from our perch on the low slung roof of one of the lumber sheds. Legs had brought his Cooey .22 rifle and had asked to take part in the drill, but Pearkes said he didn't want any wise-ass kid messing up his training program.

Legs' real first name was Edward but, except for his parents, the teachers, and their Baptist minister, nobody called him that. Like every other boy he had a nickname. And, like all the others, it was based on self evident logic.

Tommy Simmons had the chore of carrying out the ashes from the family wood heater every morning before school, so he was christened "Ashcan". Ralph Clelland possessed a talent the rest of us envied. He could squirt a four foot arch of saliva through a narrow gap in his front teeth. As a consequence, he was known as "Spit". Legs got his nickname by hanging around with Joey Froget, who was of course called "Frog". That his side kick had to be called "Legs", was as natural as sunrise and sunset.

Legs was a few years older than I, and ahead of me in school. But after Frog's family moved away we became good friends. He was, in retrospect, something of an intellectual and a lot smarter than he let on. His grades, which could have been out-standing, were merely adequate. His homework was never done. Yet, the stack of books in his bedroom belied his feigned dislike of reading. When a British pilot force-landed his train-ing plane near our school, Miss Portman asked him to come in and give us a talk about England. He asked for a volunteer to draw a map of the United Kingdom on the blackboard. Legs was the only one who could do it from memory.

His name was appropriate. His legs and arms were long and spindly. He was an awkward skater, couldn't catch or throw a ball, and only took part in compulsory sporting events orga-nized by the teachers. His ichabodish appearance, and his family's poverty (they lived in a converted church on the out-skirts of town) made Legs something of an outcast. At the very

54

least, he wasn't popular. But he did have one thing going for him. He was a great shot. As Frog used to say, he could shoot the kneecaps off a gnat at fifty paces. The fact that Legs once shot Frog in the heel at one pace while they were walking single file hunting rabbits, in no way diminished his praise for Legs' marksmanship.

Legs also seemed to know everything that went on around town ... which kids crowding around the ice cream counter at the Chinaman's were legitimate and which were of questionable pedigree. Whatever anyone thought of him, you couldn't, in the lingo of the time, "bull" him. He knew a naked emperor when he saw one and said so. Maybe that's why John Pearkes had no use for him.

It was getting dark. Pearkes stood up, tried to suck in his ample belly, and whacked the riding crop he'd been carrying against the side of his faded khaki breeches.

"Alright men, I'm going to be turning in. See you here Wednesday, 2000 hours. Meantime, remember, before this thing is over we have to face the possibility that some of us here may have to lay down our lives for King and Country. And there's no guarantee that we won't have Krauts marching around right here in Kirkcaldy."

"They're already here," someone piped up from the back. Pearkes cast a quizzical look in the direction of the voice.

"Ten Kraut families ... forners ... already livin' here", another voice chimed in.

"They're not Germans. They're Mennonites from Russia." I recognized Duke's voice. He spoke with an English accent.

"Well," said the first voice, "they look like Germans, they act like Germans, and they talk German. That makes them German in my books."

"If ya ask me," the second voice continued, "they's reportin' straight to Hitler an' gettin' paid fer it. Where else is they gettin' all that money they got fer buyin' tractors an' cars?"

"That's right," said the first voice, "Ben Froese got himself a new tractor last fall while all his neighbors is working horses. Now, I see him driving around in a '34 Chevy."

"I hear he's got a pitcher of the Fuehrer hangin' on the wall in his kitchen," said voice number two. "Got the King on t'other side and jes switches her over when one o' us drops by."

"I say we go torch his barn," the first voice said.

Pearkes tapped the riding crop gently into the palm of his left hand. "We'll have none of that, men. This is going to be a disciplined unit. But, keep your eyes peeled. Watch out for saboteurs and report anything suspicious to me."

"What a pile of horse manure," Legs muttered under his breath. "Let's go to the Chinaman's for a coca cola."

Pearkes got a good turnout the following Wednesday, but on Saturday only half of his men showed up. He decided to cut the march short. Instead of circling the entire sports field, the unit would make a sharp left approximately in line with second base on the big ball diamond, proceed to the third baseline bleachers, then cut a sharp angle to the main gate to avoid the curve and incline at the concession stands which were still giving the marchers no end of trouble.

Back at the rendezvous point, it was discovered that Big Bob Murdoch, who had been put in charge of "refreshments" was a no show. He'd last been seen at the Licensed Premises in St. Lambert that afternoon. It should be said, in Big Bob's favor, that he had offered to bring several jars of his own brew, but this generous offer had been gratefully declined by his more discerning brothers in arms.

The next training night, only six men answered the roll call. Pearkes announced that operations would be suspended during the hot month of August, and resume on the first Saturday after the Labor Day weekend. They never were.

But, his words turned out to be more prophetic than anyone had thought. German soldiers did walk the streets of Kirkcaldy. Three of them. Freimut, Dieter and Lothar, clad in dark blue prisoner of war coveralls with a big red bulls-eye on the back, arrived as harvest laborers at the end of the war. Much to their relief, they were all assigned to Mennonite farms where they could converse in German.

Freimut worked for the Friesens, our neighbors on one side, Dieter and Lothar at the Kroekers on the other. Freimut was a tall, rangy Bavarian of about nineteen. Every Sunday, he would don his Luftwaffe uniform, at least what he had left of it after being shot down over Normandy. He was careful to explain that he did so not out of any particular loyalty to the Nazis, but because the uniform was the closest thing he had to dress clothes.

56

He was the son of a school teacher, and had never done a lick of physical work in his life. He did his best to keep it that way. It was easy to spot his rack in the field. It was the one heading to the threshing machine with a poorly stacked load trailing sheaves behind it. His team's reins hung slack, leaving the horses to find their own way to the threshing outfit.

Dieter, on the other hand, was short and muscular. He'd been a steel worker before ending up in Rommel's Afrika Korps. He was tough as nails, and after three years as a POW he was still a bitter and angry man. He was angry with his Canadian prison guards. He railed against the *verfluchte Italiener* who he said couldn't fight worth a damn. He wasn't any kinder to Hitler whom he blamed for Rommel's defeat in the desert.

His plan was, that as soon as he got back to Germany, he would start the necessary paperwork to begin a new life in South Africa. Only half in jest, he said he might stop off in England to find the British officer who had captured him at El Alamein and beat the hell out of him - not for capturing him but for throwing a bucket of piss in his face when he asked for water. His bitterness blinded him to his blessings. He had come out of the war unscathed. The British officer in question may not have.

Although Dieter bunked with Lothar, or because of it, they didn't get along. The men were polar opposites. Lothar was as pious as Dieter was profane. He read his Bible every night and knelt to say his prayers before going to bed, "like a little six year old," Dieter jeered.

It had been a sunny August day in France in 1944 when Lothar hitched his old plowhorse to a cart, both of which had been requisitioned from a French farmer, and did what he did every afternoon ... fetch two barrels of water from a nearby well for his army field kitchen. He was ahead of schedule, and decided to take a nap on the shade side of the cart. He was awakened by a sharp jab in the chest. He looked up to see two Canadian soldiers, bayonets fixed, motioning him to get up. Lothar's war was over.

Of the three, Lothar was the only one to attend the Mennonite Sunday church service. And it was at church where this kindly bumbling man ran head on into rock-ribbed Mennonite theology. It happened on a communion Sunday. Anyone at this

57

service who had not been baptized into the Brethren faith (immersion), or whose spiritual credentials might in any way be suspect, quietly slipped out the door just before the Lord's Supper got under way. Lothar stayed. The appropriate passage from I Corinthians was read a second time, in German.

> *Whosoever eats the bread or drinks the cup of the*
> *Lord in an unworthy manner shall be guilty of the*
> *body and blood of the Lord.*

Lothar stayed put. This Wehrmacht warrior obviously had blood on his hands, and by any yardstick manifestly unfit to partake of the symbolic body and blood of Christ with the truly worthy. Blasphemy. Sacrilege. But partake he did.

An embarrassed Brother Kroeker tried to explain to the other Brethren, who were absolutely certain of their moral correctness, that Lothar had done so out of ignorance not malice, and thus God would not hold him accountable for this sin. Brother Doerksen was not persuaded. Such a thing, he declared emphatically, must never happen again.

It never did. By the time the next monthly communion service rolled around, the harvest was over, and Lothar was gone.

Sadly, another of John Pearkes' patriotic ramblings turned out to be prescient. Trooper Edward McCreary had fought his way through the mud of the Scheldt where the Germans had blown the dikes. He had been cheered in the Canadian Army's triumphant march through liberated Amsterdam. Spring of 1945 found his unit pushing into northern Germany and across the Ems River. Early one morning, a German sniper found Legs, sitting on a tank, in the cross-hairs of his rifle scope. It was April 25th. In thirteen days the war would be over. He is buried in a Canadian War Cemetery at the edge of a Dutch pine forest near the German frontier. He was nineteen.

I long ago lost a hound, a bay horse and
a turtle dove, and am still on their trail

— Henry David Thoreau

THE GOSPEL ACCORDING TO DUKE

Nobody around Kirkcaldy ever called him by his inflated moniker. Everyone knew him as Duke. Wellington Legget-Bourke was a remittance man. At the age of eighteen his parents in England had paid him to leave the country to live in Canada, Australia, or any other British colony that would have him. Anywhere except England. He chose Canada, specifically the Prairies.

Exactly what dirty deed he had done to deserve banishment wasn't known. What was known was that there were thousands of young Englishmen just like him. Duke was well educated and well read. He had, at one time in his life, been drawn to the stage. He had a rich bass baritone voice which he shared precisely once a year with the farm folk around Kirkcaldy. Every December he attended the Christmas Tree concert at the Duval country school near our farm. (Although he was a bachelor, he served on the school board). After Mary, Joseph, and all the little shepherds had taken off their bedsheets for another year, and the wax candles on the tree were lit, Duke led the assembly in the singing of *Good King Wenceslas*, *O Come All Ye Faithful* and the other well known carols.

After allowing for decent coaxing time, Mildred Dingwall would slide onto the piano stool. That was Duke's cue to belt out something from Gilbert and Sullivan or *The Road to Mandalay*. The crowd always demanded an encore, and that encore inevitably was what they were all waiting for; Duke's rendition of *Asleep in the Deep*. The evening ended with the singing of a somewhat mournful rendition of *Silent Night*.

When Duke sang, there was no sign of his British stutter which seems as much a part of English aristocracy as tweeds and brogues, although I never saw him wear either. The only other time Duke didn't stutter was when he'd had a few drinks.

He had come to Manitoba by way of Alberta. He had heard that one of Charles Dickens' sons had once made a new life for himself with the Northwest Mounted Police. So he decided, or more accurately his parents decided for him, to come to the

West and make a fresh start.

By the time he got there, and for some reason Duke equated the West with a place called Alberta, Dickens' son had long since been drummed out of the Force for drunkenness. Getting into the "mounties" wasn't as easy for adventurous English lads as it had once been. Besides, Duke's feet were, by his own admission, flatter than piss on a plate. And, as he got older, his bunions grew so big he had to have his shoes custom made. But he was, nevertheless, a first class horseman. After the mounties turned him down, he worked for some of the biggest cattle outfits in the foothills around Black Diamond and Pincher before filing on a homestead at Kirkcaldy. It was a bushy quarter not far from the farm we'd eventually live on. Here, he bred the finest Quarter Horses and Arabians for miles around.

It was because of his bad feet that I got to know Duke a lot better than I otherwise would have. He needed help with work that called for being on your feet a lot, and on a farm that's just about everything. As a teenager, when I wasn't busy on my stepfather's farm, I'd help out Duke hoeing potatoes, cleaning out the barn, grooming the horses, and stooking his oats on the only bit of land he bothered to cultivate. The rest of his farm was heavily wooded, mostly poplar, except for open patches of meadow where he grazed his horses. Whitetail deer were numerous, and provided him with fresh venison summer and winter.

And this was one of the drawbacks working for Duke. He served venison two times a day. Venison roasted, scorched, broiled, fried, stewed, and in sausages. It landed on the table seven days a week, sometimes hot, sometimes cold, but always unmistakably deer meat. Breakfast also never varied. Always the same brain-like glob of gray porridge; not quite hot, not quite cold. The only respite from this fare came when one of the neighbour ladies, Mrs. Davis or Mrs. North, brought over a freshly baked apple or saskatoon berry pie.

One particularly chilly day while helping Duke put new tar paper on the west wall of his shack, he proudly announced that he'd made some Yorkshire pudding to go with the venison roast. For me, it was to be another culinary disappointment. Yorkshire pudding, I soon discovered, bears about as much resemblance to pudding as Mennonite sausage does to cheesecake.

If Duke ever took a bath, it was one of his better kept secrets. A complicated smell moved with him like an aura wherever he went. It was a mixture redolent of horse sweat, damp manure, stale tea leaves, carbolic disinfectant, (used to castrate colts), and the unmistakable heavy odour of human perspiration.

After every meal he wiped his hands on the bib of his overalls which, over time, had taken on the glossy, black appearance of newly mined coal. Like our other English neighbours, he had a peculiar way of eating. He pushed the food onto his knife, then stacked it onto the arch of the fork before precariously aiming it toward his mouth.

Unlike our other English neighbours, Duke always said grace before meals. And when the student minister opened the Kirkcaldy Anglican Church for the summer months, Duke rarely missed a Sunday.

So, I was surprised, perhaps shocked would be a better word, when Duke bared his religious philosophy one evening during supper after a hard day pounding fence posts. While Duke was reciting grace, I solemnly stared down at the venison steak on my plate which looked about as appetizing as burnt brake lining. His booming "amen" was my cue to reach for the steak knife which I hoped would be sharp enough to handle the task at hand.

"I don't know why I bother with this nonsense," Duke thundered without provocation.

"It's lots of work, but I can't see you without horses." I presumed he was referring to the fencing work.

"I'm not talking about my bloody horses," Duke shot back. "I'm talking about all this bowing and scraping we do before the Almighty we've been taught to do since we were knee high to a grasshopper." He paused, then went on. "Ever wonder what kind of God has such a low opinion of Himself, or such a colossal ego that His creatures have to constantly tell Him how great and wonderful He is ... praising Him here, honoring Him there. If you ask me the Creator, whoever He is, can't even control what He's made. This whole universe we live in is one big crap shoot."

I froze on my chair. At any second I expected a thunderbolt

to slice through the leaky roof of Duke's lean-to kitchen. I did not take the possibility of such an event lightly, and for good reason. It had happened earlier that summer. I was bringing the milk cows home from the back pasture over some freshly worked summerfallow. I was puzzled why my usually placid horse was so jumpy, and the herd unusually restless. The day had been a scorcher and I was slouched on my horse, daydreaming. To be honest, my thoughts were wandering, like a young boy's will, into what my Sunday School teacher referred to as "forbidden areas." Mr. Rempel constantly warned us boys against certain thoughts ... impure thoughts.

It was late afternoon, but the claustrophobic heat of the day had not yet subsided. Then it happened. The air crackled. A flash out of a clear sky, then a deafening bang. It felt like the earth itself was being ripped apart. My horse sank to her knees. The cattle stampeded. Then, deathly stillness. Through my blurred vision I watched a small curl of white smoke rising from a blackened stone no more than fifteen feet to my right. God had spared me. This time.

Duke gave me an indulgent smile when I told him the story, but said nothing. He pulled a blue polka dotted handkerchief the size of a small tea towel out of his back pocket, and swiped it across his perpetually dripping nose which, over the years, had turned red as raw meat. As a born again Christian, I felt this was the moment to witness.

"Yes," I said, "we praise Him because He is the giver of all good things. He is the God of love who sent his only Son to earth to save us and give us everlasting life. And, He provides for us here on earth."

"Does He now," Duke said with a sneer. "If, He provides why were we killing ourselves pounding posts today, and tomorrow we'll be burning our hides to a crisp stacking hay? And in a few months we'll be hauling firewood out of the bush. You know why? So we bloody well don't freeze to death this winter, that's why." Duke pushed his plate away and fumbled his pipe out of a side pocket. "Yes," he went on, "maybe God keeps His eye on the sparrow, like the Good Book says, but us? Well, let's just say He looks after those of us who look after themselves."

Duke gave a loud laugh and started shoving a fresh load of Old Chum into his pipe. He used a small tamper to make sure the tobacco would draw properly, not too loose and not too firm. He then snapped the white tip of a wooden match against his twisted thumb nail and held the flame at arm's length until the sulphur burned off. Then, with the flourish of a symphony conductor he brought the match over the bowl making short, rapid puffs to get a burn started. This accomplished, he blew a long column of white smoke toward the fly-specked ceiling. There he rested his eyes as if seeking divine inspiration.

It was his ritual prelude to some profound words of wisdom that were formulating in his mind about to be pronounced to a waiting world. In this case the world was me and Rivers, Duke's mongrel, lying snoring under the table.

"When your God put man in charge of creation," he said, still staring at the ceiling, "He made a damn poor choice now, didn't He?" Duke didn't seem to be waiting for an answer, so I said nothing. In any event, I had no answer.

"You know, there's nobody as selfish as a Christian. At least what passes for a Christian. Thinks this planet is his own little candy store God made just for him because he's such a special fellow."

"Well, I don't know about that." I said, "but I do know the Bible tells us to be good stewards of the land."

"That it does, that it does," Duke replied in a magisterial tone of voice. He got up and pulled a half full 26 of Beefeater gin from the kitchen cupboard. Slowly he poured three fingers into a near-empty glass of what I had taken to be water.

"Yes, says right there in Genesis. Your God didn't just put old Adam and Eve in a beautiful garden, he commanded them to nurture and keep it, now didn't He?"

Duke's Adam's apple bobbed up, and then down, as he took a tight-lipped swallow of neat gin. "But," he continued, "you 'born agains' can't think of anything except being fruitful and multiplying." He suddenly roared with laughter, and just as suddenly turned serious again. "Ever read the Bible where it tells you to be at peace with the birds of the air and the animals of the field? About how you're even supposed to be careful how you move stones and the good Lord knows he gave us plenty of those." Duke slapped the side of his leg, and laughed loudly.

"But Duke," I protested, "you shoot deer out of season all year round and eat them."

"Sure," he countered somewhat defensively, "but I also let them feed off my haystacks in winter when they're up to their puckered little sphincters in snow and can't get at the grass. Not like old man Sawatsky who guns them down and feeds them to his dogs."

"Yeh," I conceded, "Mr. Sawatsky is on the cheap side alright."

"Cheap be damned. He's a no good, low down miser. Tighter than a bear's asshole at chokecherry time."

I suppressed a chuckle. The farther the gin dropped in his glass, the more florid and scatological Duke's vocabulary became.

"That old bugger Sawatsky, and he's a lay preacher, or deacon or something in your church is he not?"

"Yeh, he's a deacon."

"There you go. A deacon and he breaks every square inch of land he can squeeze a plow into. Why just last summer, what does he do? Drains the slough on his last wood lot and bull-dozes every damn tree so as he can get himself a few more bushels of wheat. Think your God likes that?" Duke tipped the bottle toward the glass, slopping some gin on the table.

"Duke, why do you always say 'your God.' He's yours too, isn't He? You go to the Anglican church when your preacher's in town. Don't you pray to the same God as us Mennonites do?"

"Let me tell you something. No, on second thought you tell me. Do you think everybody that goes to church is a believer? Found the truth for now and evermore? Nothing as dangerous as the person that's found the truth with a capital T, you know."

Rivers stirred, and ambled his arthritic frame towards the screen door. Without getting up, Duke pushed the door open with his right foot, waited until the dog was out, then let it slap shut again.

Again he stared up at the ceiling. "Knew a woman once who'd found the truth. I was riding Apache back from the big fall roundup at the Double D at Pincher. Ever tell you about Apache?"

"Yeh, your favorite horse."

"Let me tell you. I've seen a lot of fine horse flesh in my day. Nothing will ever touch Apache ... I tell you, maybe God didn't make anything perfect, but he came about as damn close as you can get when he made Apache.

"Then the sleeping sickness hit. Only horse in our bunch that got it. Had him lying in the corral in a coma for two weeks. Wasted away to nothing but a bunch of bones wrapped in hide." Duke took a swallow, pursed his lips, and gave a slight shudder as the alcohol bit into his throat. The bottle now stayed on the table. For the last two drinks he hadn't bothered to put it back in the cupboard.

He stared up at the ceiling again before speaking. "One night I belted down half a glass straight, took the sharpest butcher knife I could find in the bunkhouse kitchen, went out and cut his throat. Hardest goddamn thing I ever did."

Duke turned his face and stared out the cob-webbed kitchen window. Rivulets of tears slowly worked their way through the deep crevices of his face, and disappeared in a week's growth of graying whiskers.

"But what about the woman who had found the truth?" I asked, in an effort to get him off the painful subject of Apache. Duke cleared his throat in an exaggerated sort of way before answering.

"Oh, her. Well, as I was saying, Apache and I were on our way back from the Double D when I ran into this Sarah Pettigrew, handsome enough young woman I might say, but all addled up with religion. Anyway, she's heading down the South Range Road with her horse and buggy peddling her pamphlets."

"Jehovah's Witness?"

"Yes. Well, she lit into me about the Second Coming and how I still had a chance to change my ways, and about some big battle called Armageddon that was going to be fought in the desert somewhere, and something about my soul's eternal tomorrow."

"So, what did you tell her?" I asked, barely able to suppress a smile. I was on safe ground here. Scoffing at "Witnesses" whose doctrine was ridiculed in our church, and by every Mennonite I knew, was quite acceptable. Yet I was both puzzled and disturbed by the increasing numbers of Mennonites who were embracing this sect even though God had blessed them with a faith, that like Duke's horse, was about as close to perfection as you could get.

"What did I tell her, you ask? Told her a joke. Well, maybe it wasn't a joke. I said, 'Mrs. Pettigrew, I don't even believe in my own religion ... and it happens to be the true faith.' 'Mr. Legget-Bourke,' she snapped, 'if you are half as wise as you think you are you'll give some thought to your tomorrow ..' Well, with that she hauled out her buggy whip, gave her nag a whack across the arse and took off like a bat out of hell. Never talked to me again."

Duke arose from the table, stood parade-square erect and screwed the cap on the bottle. He did so with elaborate care, like a mechanic putting a nut on a bolt careful not to strip the thread. With an uncertain gait he approached the cupboard, opened it with a ceremonial flourish, and put the bottle back. He sat down heavily, fixing his eyes on the ceiling again. "By the way," he asked, "when the lightning hit that stone fifteen feet from where you were riding." He stopped abruptly. His mind suddenly seemed to be elsewhere.

"Yeh?" I said.

"As I was saying, when the lightning hit near where you were riding, let's say you'd been right on top of that stone instead of where you were, do you think God would have moved that lightning bolt over some to spare your life?"

"Could of if He'd wanted to," I countered somewhat defensively.

Duke funnelled the last few drops of gin left in his glass down his throat and got up out of his chair. "Well, what the hell," he said smiling, "how He gets us doesn't matter a damn. But, mark my words, one way or the other He's going to get us. Bet on it."

It would be ten years before our paths crossed again. While I'd been away at Bible School my parents left the Kirkcaldy farm and moved to a larger Mennonite community. I had no reason to return, yet as I matured, I was drawn back. Was it to seek confirmation of a place that had been such an inextricable part of my childhood? Was it to reaffirm memories of people I had known before they slipped into some kind of fantasy world?

Much had changed. Our old farmstead had been demolished, the victim of a new owner's greed and the bulldozer's blade. Green stalks of wheat caressed the very edge of the road where a row of lilacs once unabashedly poured their Evening in Paris fragrance into the blue prairie sky. To my dismay, the Manitoba

Maple shelter belt had been pushed up into a grotesque pile of mangled roots and branches. One lone tree had survived the mayhem to grow defiantly from the very top of the mound. I resisted the temptation to look for broken pieces of dishes and glass which I knew were there, and which I would immediately recognize.

Smells of mid summer decay filled the sloughs graced by wary mother mallards with strings of fluffy progeny in tow.

I headed for Duke's place. His farm had the sad look of impending departure about it. It had grown unfamiliar by time. The tangle of scrap iron, once overgrown with ragweed and sow thistle behind his shack, was now stacked in a neat conical pile beside the stable. Rusty plow shares, cast iron seats from horse drawn hay mowers, twisted cultivator frames ... all waiting for the salvage truck. The little usable machinery still on the place was lined up in a straight row along the fence dividing the yard and the oat field, which had reverted to pasture, mostly quack grass.

Five horses, all on the lean side, jerked up their heads and came snorting to the fence to check the credentials of the intruder. A cardboard sign nailed to a gatepost at the road leading into the farm announced the date and the time of the auction. Duke was nowhere in sight.

With a handful of sage pressed to my nostrils, I breathed its medicinal aroma in deeply. I looked east, beyond the main pasture, past the woodlot where Duke and I had cut countless cords of firewood, to the crown grazing lands that rose pale and gently into the horizon. I could make out a solitary, ambling figure clambering to the top of an outcropping of rock, stand erect, then scan the high ground that falls precipitously into the valley below.

"Thought that might be you, Duke," I half shouted against the wind that inflated my lungs the instant I opened my mouth. Duke fixed his deep-set blue eyes on me with an unseeing stare. Time had stolen their mischievous twinkle, and had carved even deeper crevices into his sun blasted face.

My expectant smile searched for recognition but found none. "What are you looking for, old friend?" I asked, as I sheepishly lowered my proffered but ungrasped hand.

"Apache, my sorrel," he said at last. "Need him for the

roundup at the Double D at Pincher."

"Apache? Round up at Pincher? Duke, Apache's ...." The strong wind rammed the words back into my throat. Duke's watery eyes remained fixed on the horizon.

"Saw him here on the rise but yesterday. Can't figure where he could have gotten to."

"Tell you what Duke, let's call 'er a day. He can't have gone far. Let's go have a cup of tea. I'll help you take another look tomorrow."

"Yes, tomorrow," Duke murmured. "We'll take another look tomorrow. A cuppa tea. Tomorrow."

La donna e` mobile

— from Rigoletto
by Verdi

HOLD MY CIGARETTE

I was sixteen, in love with an older woman of eighteen. A whisker short of six feet, I was a boy in a man's frame, all bones and bad skin. She was everything I was not. Olive complexioned, self assured, sophisticated.

We met one noon hour in the rink shack, I on my lunch break from class, she visiting her parents on a winter break from a private Catholic girls' school in the States. Skating among my female classmates, she stood out like a rose in a bouquet of petunias. While the local girls stockings were all lumpy, covering long underwear I presumed, she wore a short plaid skirt over black tights which accentuated her long shapely legs. Her hair was jet black, cut like a boy's. It seemed to be sculpted on her head. She smiled easily, a dazzling white smile wrapped in raspberry red lips.

Momentarily losing her balance, she sat down heavily beside me on the shack bench to tighten her skate laces. She picked at them gingerly with long, burnished, jelly bean-pink fingernails.

"Here," she said matter of factly, lifting an elegant leg across my knee, "you're probably better at this. Oh, my name's Kathleen, everybody calls me Kathy. What's yours?"

For a few seconds, that seemed to stretch into eternity, I groped for my name. The clumsy introduction over, I began loosening her laces. It was as close to intimacy as I'd ever come. I pulled each set of eyelets tight, working my way carefully from bottom to top.

"Ah, that's better." She fairly breathed the words as she shifted her weight, and arced the other gam across my lap.

"You're a pretty good skater," she said, as she stamped her feet on the wooden floor to test the firmness of her newly tightened skates.

"Not too bad," I replied, with typical Canadian modesty.

"Well," she said, shooting out a mittened hand, "why don't we go for a whirl. There's no music, but the way you skate we don't need any."

My knees felt like marshmallows, and I wasn't at all sure I

could make it around the rink with the grace and style obviously expected of me. Furthermore, I didn't know where, or how, to hold her. I had never skated with a partner before. I placed my right hand in her left and began circling the rink.

"Not like that," she laughed, wrapping my right arm around her waist.

I needn't have worried about finding something to talk about during the skate. Conversation came easily to her, and she seemed genuinely interested in me.

On the second corner we were up to speed. She cut her outside skate hard, but effortlessly, sending up a white rooster tail of slivered ice. For one electrifying second our thighs touched.

I'll bet you're a good dancer too," she said, as we repeated the touch and lift off manoeuvre on the next curve.

"D..d...dancing?" I stammered. "Well, you see, we don't....I mean, I don't right now. Too much homework, have to help Dad on the farm you know."

"There's a dance tomorrow night at the Odd Fellows Hall. It's Saturday. You should come."

"Well, I'll try," knowing full well that being allowed to go to a dance was about as likely as getting a call from Hollywood.

"Phew! time for a break," she said, as she leaned against me with exaggerated exhaustion. Her closeness gave off a fragrance just like the cosmetic counter at Eaton's department store in Brandon.

"Care for a smoke?" she asked, tugging a flat pack of Black Cats from a jacket pocket.

"Eh, no thanks."

"These Canadian cigarette packages are so awkward to handle," she complained, "and your smokes are so mild. I'm out of Camels, so I guess these'll have to do." She lit a Black Cat and inhaled deeply. "You don't smoke at all?"she asked.

"Well,er,no. Well, not now, I kinda feel a cold coming on. Decided to hold off for a while."

She parted her lips slowly, took the cigarette from her mouth, and handed it to me.

"Here," she said, "hold my cigarette." I slipped the burning cigarette between the fore and middle fingers of my right hand like a seasoned smoker, even though the closest I'd come to taking up the habit was trying to smoke dry maple leaves wrapped in newsprint when I was twelve. While I held her cigarette, she straightened her tights by running her cupped hands along her calves in a massaging motion.

We were the last skaters off the ice. As we returned to the shack, it seemed as though we had known each other all our lives. However, I knew a lot more about her than she about me. Her parents were Tom and Mabel Kennedy, the lumber yard Kennedys. Mrs. Kennedy was a painfully shy woman. The townsfolk said she rarely left the house because she had bad nerves. Mr. Kennedy, by contrast, was an outgoing, talkative man who spoke with, what some said, was an Irish lilt. He would listen patiently as my father tried to explain that he wanted "tvinty-tree zwei b' fohrs."

I had always assumed that Tom and Mabel were childless. And, in a way, they were. Kathy was six when her mother had been hospitalized, and she had gone to live with her Aunt May in Minneapolis. What was to have been a temporary stay, turned out to be permanent, except for infrequent visits to see her parents.

It was Friday, the end of the school week. The Saturday dance was, of course, out for me. Kathy and I agreed to meet for a skate Monday night when the rink's outdoor lights would be on, and her father would hook up the speaker system. We could skate to her new record by the Mills Brothers…*Glow Little Glow Worm.* Monday night didn't present a problem. I'd be back in town at the Robinsons where I boarded during the winter months.

That weekend was the longest of my life. I tried to shorten it by going to bed early on Saturday night, and by not thinking about Kathy dancing the night away at the Odd Fellows Hall.

At church the next morning, maybe I was imagining it, but I fairly felt the preacher's eyes boring through me before he lowered his eyes to read the text for his sermon.

"The scripture reading for today's message is found in Second Timothy, chapter two, verse 19", he intoned, in his customary authoritative manner.

Nevertheless, the firm foundation of God stands, having this seal, "The Lord knows those who are His, and let everyone who names the name of the Lord abstain from wickedness."

73

Had I not just named the name of the Lord by giving the closing prayer in our Sunday School class? Wicked? Well, I wasn't so sure about that. Perhaps foolish. Although, I had to admit that I was in love with someone who wore bright red lipstick, and whose make up went well beyond the accepted light powdering and faint rouge favoured by the girls in church. I had to concede too, that the smoking put Kathy well beyond the pale of Mennonite acceptability, let alone that of a professed Christian. And yes, I had held her cigarette, even if I hadn't smoked it. And, although I hadn't actually lied, I had shaved the truth pretty close when I told her I'd like to go on to university to study law, when I knew perfectly well I'd promised my mother I'd go to Bible School after High School and give the ministry serious consideration. None of this, I reasoned, could be pleasing in the sight of the Lord. I was definitely starting to color outside the lines.

Whatever pangs of conscience I felt in church on Sunday were gone by Monday. The lights of Paris or Broadway never shone brighter than the sixty watt bulbs strung over the town skating rink that Monday night. Clusters of younger kids sliding around on the sides of their skates, were already on the ice.

I hadn't expected Kathy to be there so early. I hadn't expected Doug Maxwell to be there at all. Doug had been one of the "big boys" when I was in the lower grades, and was now at university studying agriculture.

"Hi," Kathy shouted from the dark end of the shack when I walked in. "Missed you at the dance. We had a super time."

"Yeh, sure did," Doug said, as he sat down beside her. "Would've had an even better time if the beer hadn't run out so soon," he added, with a conspiratorial whisper. Kathy gave him a friendly poke in the ribs and lit a Black Cat, then said, "Dougie, be a dear and hold my cigarette."

I laced my skates, missed an eyelet, undid them and laced them up again. At last Kathy and Doug steadied each other onto the ice. My opening to make an exit.

I hadn't noticed how dark and cold it was. It was one of those winter nights when the smoke from the chimneys goes up straight and white, and the air is so stunningly still. So still, that when I opened the front door at the Robinsons, fragments of the perfectly synchronized voices of the Mills Brothers were still wafting through the air.

> *glow little glow worm*
> *glimmer, glimmer.......*
> *turn on the AC and the DC.......*
> *......and lead us on to love.*

Unless you can learn to forgive your parents, you can never grow up

— *Anonymous*

BURYING MY FATHER

My father, or more precisely my stepfather, was born the year Gottlieb Daimler invented the automobile, and died sixteen years after Neil Armstrong set foot on the moon. He viewed neither event with any great degree of significance, and the latter with considerable skepticism.

He entered the world in the dying days of the nineteenth century, but was never able to entirely let go of it. He felt decidedly uncomfortable in the twentieth, in which he was destined to live his entire adult life. Its technological miracles and scientific achievements failed to impress him. He would no more have thought of boarding a plane than jumping off a ten storey building, of which he saw very few.

He never owned a television set, never turned on the radio, (although he often turned it off). He declined to learn to drive a car, and continued to do the fall plowing with horses, while my brother and I worked adjoining fields with modern tractors.

He came to maturity during the Mennonite Golden Age in Russia, (Die Goldene Jahren). Neither he, nor his contemporaries, suspected that this utopian period was already in the early stages of its *Götterdämmerung*.

His family was not among the wealthiest of the German-Russian landowners, but sepia photographs show fashionably attired parents and siblings, iron-gated grounds surrounding a handsome, if not luxurious, home. The pictures speak of comfortable, middle class circumstances.

He rarely talked about his parents. I got the impression that his father had had, if not a downright mean streak, a strong tyrannical nature which may have contributed to his mother's death.

My father's purpose on this earth, as he saw it, was to live a simple, pious life that would assure him a place in heaven, and do so by spending as little money as possible. To accomplish this, children were a definite asset.

A child's role was to labor diligently in the barns and fields without remuneration, and barefoot. (Shoes were worn only in school and church.) Children were expected to spend only as much time in school as the law demanded, and to master the rudiments of sums, reading, and writing. Anything beyond that was needlessly tempting the devil, of whose visceral presence he had not the slightest doubt.

When cattle bolted through fences, he was as sure that the devil had made them do it, as he was that demons had possessed the Garasene swine.

The account of how Jesus had driven the demons from a raving lunatic and, after much begging on their part, had relented to let them enter a herd of swine, (who promptly killed themselves by jumping off a cliff), was featured prominently in his repertoire of biblical bedtime stories. The other standards included the story of The Loaves and Fishes, Jonah and the Whale, David and Goliath, Sampson and Delilah, and that no good Absalom, a juvenile delinquent who wouldn't get a proper hair cut. His vanity cost him his life when he rode his mule under an old oak tree and got his long locks caught in its branches. His mount kept right on going, leaving him hanging high and dry, so one of his father's friends took the opportunity to run him through with a spear.

In telling my sisters and me Bible stories, which he considered his Christian parental duty, he spared neither gore nor raw passion. While Miss MacIntosh, our primary teacher, read us stories about Snow White and the Seven Dwarfs, our father was into much meatier stuff; King David standing on the roof of his house watching the very married Bathsheba bathing. Lusting after her, he got her pregnant, and made her soldier-husband point man in battle to make sure he'd get killed, so he could marry his beautiful wife, and presumably live happily ever after. End of story. Bedtime.

It never occurred to my father that telling a seven year old about the Bible's most notorious adulterer would do him harm, (which it didn't). After all, the Bible was the indisputable divine word all the way from Genesis to Revelations, so who was he to censor God?

Any theology beyond these simplistic stories was problematic for him. He reverenced the itinerant preachers who came from the cities to minister to the backwoods folks, and who spoke about God as though they had a monopoly on the subject. If something they said made a particular impression on him, he would usually share it with us at morning devotions.

Every morning at breakfast, he stumbled through the mini homily he tore off the kitchen sermonette calendar. Written in High German, these readings gave him a lot of trouble. His limited vocabulary was no match for the intellect of the German theologians who had crafted these inspirational bon mots.

As soon as he cleared his throat to begin reading, his normally quite resonant voice became tight as a tin whistle. The higher the level of piety he strove to achieve, the thinner his voice became, so that I was sometimes moved to look up, convinced that a pair of invisible hands were tightening their grip around his thin, sun-scorched neck. Assured by the bobbing motion of his Adam's apple that this was not the case, I lowered my eyes to continue counting the petals on the tiny painted roses that ringed my porridge bowl.

Unlike most Mennonite fathers of his day, he avoided corporal punishment. This aversion to physical violence was, however, not shared by other members of the family. Many Mennonite parents who argued strenuously, and persuasively, for the principle of non-violence when their sons got their draft notices, nevertheless saw it as their God-given duty to beat their children to within an inch of their lives, and never sound a word of praise, in case such a gesture contribute to the sin of pride.

For my father, child labor was another matter. He saw it as his parental obligation never to allow after hours school, or sports events, to interfere with farm work.

When my sister and her husband came by to see if I could join them for a day at the Brandon Fair, the answer was an emphatic no. There was more than enough work on the farm to keep a boy out of trouble, and the frivolity of a fair was no place for a Christian to find himself anyway. Although he didn't say so, I knew he was worried that I might ask for a dollar's spending money. If such a request had ever been granted, it would have rivaled the miracles of the Gospels.

When I turned fifteen, I decided it was time for a showdown. Actually, an incident that happened about this time made the decision for me. I had sold a batch of chickens I'd bought cheap from the hatchery, and raised on threshing machine screenings, only to discover that my cheque in the sum of $25.40 had disappeared. I opened the kitchen drawer where my father kept a scribbler in which his farm income and expenses were listed. As I suspected, the cheque, made out in my name, was there.

At supper, I informed him, and anyone else who cared to listen, that the following Saturday, I would be participating in our high school curling bonspiel, and consequently unavailable for my customary weekend farm work. My father muttered something about my being an irresponsible son with a decidedly un-Christian attitude. But, he did not press the matter. All work and no play had not made me a dull boy, but it had made me a rebellious one.

Religious intolerance was part of my father's faith. Catholics worshiped idols and were doomed. Oh, the odd one might slip into heaven inspite of the church, but not because of it. He was only slightly more charitable towards any Mennonite who hadn't been baptized by immersion into the Brethren Church. A sprinkle on the head after a perfunctory declaration of faith simply didn't cut it. The MB Church, he declared, might not be right on every count, but unlike all the other churches, it had the essentials right.

Overseas evangelism interested him. Every fall, at the Thanksgiving service, he made a modest contribution to foreign missions. This concern for the heathen of Africa and India was likely enhanced by remoteness because he couldn't have cared less about the spiritual, or physical, well being of the Indians and Metis within his midst, whom he also considered to be heathen.

He often remonstrated his older brother Jacob, for his liberal outlook. And, when Jacob once suggested that he could see no great harm in Mennonite young people getting together for a bit of dancing (ein besje rom hupse), my father, sniffing the burning rubber of heresy, turned apoplectic with shock. "No Jacob," he emphatically admonished his brother, "our God does not dance."

His physical well being preoccupied him almost as much as his spiritual welfare. He ate sparingly, avoided sweets, and meticulously trimmed every trace of fat from his meat.

He brushed his teeth religiously with a mangy little tooth brush which he dipped in a solution of salt and warm water. He never visited a dentist. A troublesome tooth was worked loose with his thumb and forefinger, pried up from the gumline

80

with the small blade of his jack knife, then pulled with a pair of pliers. At the end of his life, he had enough teeth left to present an acceptable smile.

Except for a prostate operation when he was in his eighties, he only entered the doors of a hospital to visit sick friends. He exercised regularly, and while other men his age developed distended paunches, my father's stomach stayed hard and flat.

He wasn't totally opposed to bathing. Every two weeks was preferable, but once a week was tolerable. Anything more than that was not only superfluous, but flirting with vanity, and wasting water.

It was an article of faith that anyone who was not in bed by 8:30 was probably up to no good, and anyone who stayed in bed past 7 a.m. was of equally questionable character.

In spite of this strict sleeping regimen, his nights were restless. Near midnight, he would sit bolt upright in bed, and howl like a coyote. In the morning he had no recollection of bad dreams or nightmares. More often than not, he commented on what a good night's sleep he had enjoyed.

My mother attributed this nocturnal shrieking to an experience he'd had during the Russian Revolution. The story was, that as a young man he had gone to work for a farm family where he slept in the hay loft. One night, he was awakened by a band of anarchist robbers. The dog barked furiously until he was silenced by two rifle shots. After ransacking the house, from which the family had fled, the bandits took the horses from the barn, and discussed dropping a match in the hay. My father had two choices; run, and get shot in the back, or be burned alive. He was saved by the match shortage of the time. None of the bandits, presumably all smokers, wanted to waste a match on the barn. They rode off, leaving the farm buildings, and my father, intact.

This traumatic incident had somehow embedded itself in his subconscious to emerge in the form of nightmares, which his conscious mind could not recollect in the morning. Eventually, we all learned to live with these blood curdling howls, and my mother made it a point to warn overnight guests. Sometimes she forgot. On one occasion she found a visiting minister and his wife huddled by the kitchen door clutching their night clothes, debating whether they should make a run for it. They probably would have, if it hadn't been such a cold night, and if Winnipeg hadn't been more than two hundred miles away.

Perhaps because of this experience he was sensitive to suffering, and was willing to spend money to alleviate it. When, at seven, I came down with such a bad cold that I had trouble breathing my father brought home a dozen oranges especially for me. Fruit was a rare and expensive commodity during the Depression. Only some time later did I learn that he had made that special trip on a day when it was minus thirty degrees F.

Esthetics however, meant little to him. One Sunday morning a visiting minister rhapsodized over the profusion of flowers my mother had planted around the old farm house. He said something about the greatness of God's handiwork. My father remained silent for a moment, then said, " Yes, I suppose they are beautiful but unfortunately they are of no practical value."

Nothing around our farm was bought that could be hand made, or fixed on the place. Hides were tanned to make and repair harnesses. A reasonably straight birch tree served as a wagon tongue, and every used nail was straightened and reused. Although he was somewhat wooden-fingered, there was no manufacturing or repair job he wouldn't tackle to avoid purchasing a new item.

A totally uncoordinated man, he rode the gentlest of mares awkwardly and uneasily. He clawed at the air in confusion when I once tossed him a soft ball, and missed catching it by several feet. So I listened with fascination, and disbelief, when he casually informed me one day that he had been a swimmer of some renown during his youth in Russia.

"How far did you swim?" I asked, with poorly disguised skepticism.

"Well, I grew up in the Molotchna, near the Sea of Azov. There was an island, a mile, maybe a mile and a half from shore."

"You swam all the way to that island?"

"Oh yes, and back again. Sometimes twice on a Sunday afternoon."

Try as I might, I could not visualize this man, whose arms and legs seemed to take off in all directions when he walked, as a graceful figure gliding through water.

He allowed a sense of humor to surface from time to time, as long as the subject wasn't his faith or money. He chuckled for days when I accidentally got my mother's chickens drunk. A pail of chokecherry pulp left over after she had extracted the juice by boiling the tart wild fruit in water and sugar, had collected some rain water. Sitting outside under a hot sun, the fermentation process was well under way by the time I decided to give the chickens a treat. Within an hour, a hundred Plymouth Rocks were staggering around the farm yard in various stages of stupification. Some stared blankly into space, others snoozed, propped up on one wing like an invalid leaning on a crutch.

My mother was not amused. Egg production for the day dropped to near zero. The hens who were inclined to lay inspite of the circumstances, couldn't make it up to the nesting boxes nailed to the hen house walls. They dropped their eggs all over the yard, where they were immediately devoured by my dog.

I last saw my father when he was nearing his one hundredth birthday. I had returned from the East, to live on the prairies again. I found him sitting alone in the living room of the city home he had shared with my mother, after they retired from the farm. The drapes were tightly drawn in the mid afternoon of a glorious autumn day. He seemed distant, and showed little enthusiasm for my visit, even though I hadn't seen him since my mother's funeral five years earlier.

He did ask me whether I was still talking on the radio. He neither condemned nor condoned my career as a broadcast journalist, but my work had always puzzled him. What events were of such earth shattering urgency, he would ask, that required me to fly all over the world and talk about them on radio and TV? And, who was paying me to do this? More importantly, why?

One wall of the darkened room was covered with a randomly assembled gallery of photographs .... parents, brothers, sisters; all were familiar to me save one. It was of a young man in a czarist military uniform. My father explained that the photo was of his oldest brother Heinrich, who had perished at the front in the First World War. It was his fervent prayer that Heinrich had, at the last moment, found grace in the eyes of the Lord, so that when my father came face to face in Heaven with all the other people in the pictures, the family circle would be intact. There was a picture of his first wife who had died in middle age and bore him no children. There was no picture of my mother, with whom he had a daughter.

Much was said at his funeral about how we were gathered, not to mourn, but to celebrate the passing of a man who, like his biblical hero Job, had lived an exemplary life full of many days. Indeed, his self-authored obituary read like Job's affirmation of his own righteousness. My mother, who had been a presence in his life for nearly fifty years, was given passing mention. Yes, she was tough to be with, sometimes impossible, but she deserved better. He also found it difficult to be generous to the children she had brought with her into the marriage, and had helped him rise from poverty to prosperity.

Conflicting emotions went tramping through my mind as I accompanied him to his final resting place. At one moment, I wanted to vent my anger like the young man who rebuked the self-righteous Job.

The abundant in years may not be wise
Nor my elders understand justice.

Then, the ephemeral fragments of another quote rattled around in my brain, only to evaporate without taking concrete form.

Every son of man travels an unbeaten
path .... footsteps judged ...

Was it from the Bible? St. Paul perhaps?

Years later, while rummaging through the remainder bin in a mall bookstore, I picked up William L. Shirer's 20th Century Journey, the journalist-historian's memoirs. And there it was, on the very first page. No, it wasn't from the Bible. It was by Clarence Darrow, the American trial lawyer who had defended the Tennessee school teacher charged with teaching evolution.

Every son of man travels an unbeaten path, a road beset with
dangers and temptations that no other wanderer met. His
footsteps can be judged only in the full knowledge of the
strength and light he had, the burden he carried, the obstacles
he met, and a thorough knowledge of every open and secret
motive that impelled him.

I closed the book. At long last, I had buried my father.

What is the good of a road if it does
not lead to a temple

— from the film 'Repentance'

A MOST PERFECT DAY

Corny and Tina Krahn did what every Kirkcaldy Mennonite couple did when the man turned 65. They retired. Stopped working. Childless, they sold the farm and moved into a modest house surrounded by five acres on the outskirts of Warden beside other retirees, who also kept a cow and a few chickens on their acreages.

Corny didn't give up his life-long love of farming for health reasons. Actually, neither he nor Tina had ever been sick a day in their lives. Maybe a touch of the flu now and again, or the occasional sniffle, but nothing serious. Certainly nothing a glass of Edelkreuter wouldn't cure. Tina, a spare, high strung woman, didn't care much for the Swiss herbal mixture, but Corny ordered it by the case through an advertisement in the German language weekly, *Der Botschafter*.

Yet at 65, when it comes to your health all bets are off, Corny reasoned. Those big companies don't make you quit working the day the old odometer clicks over to the magic number for nothing. And the government wouldn't start sending out pension cheques and paying for drug prescriptions if it didn't think it prudent for its senior citizens to drop what they're doing before they drop dead. Besides, Corny thought, retirement would give him more time to think of his spiritual, as well as his physical well being. And mortality was something Corny became increasingly conscious of after he retired.

Now that he was officially a senior, Corny thought it wise to move to a larger town close to good doctors and a hospital. Not that he was afraid of leaving this earth. He was a devout Christian who believed with all his heart that when the trumpet of the Lord sounded the dead in Christ would rise, followed by the saved still on earth, to meet Him in the sky. He was so certain of this that he ordered a bumper sticker offered on the Fargo radio station by Brother Ellsworth Carlson to anyone who sent in a love offering to his radio ministry. It read, IN CASE OF RAPTURE THIS CAR IS UNMANNED.

What kind of mayhem that might cause if he happened to be driving on a busy highway or, heaven forbid, approaching a school bus at the precise moment of rapture never entered his mind.

While Corny stood on rock solid biblical ground on this score, Tina was less sure. Except in her silent prayers she never breathed a word about her doubts to anyone; not even her husband in whom she confided on every other matter.

As soon as they settled down to the serious business of retirement, Corny transferred their church membership from the dwindling congregation at Kirkcaldy to the larger Mennonite church in Warden, sent out change of address notices and made an appointment with the doctor. In spite of urgings from her husband to make an appointment too (they're free he kept telling her), Tina demurred. She didn't think it made much sense to see a doctor if she wasn't sick. There was nothing wrong with Corny either, but he thought it prudent to get regular assurances from a doctor that he was, in fact, feeling fine.

Perched on the edge of the examination table Corny clutched the skimpy gown he had been given and tugged it over his knees while waiting anxiously for the doctor's verdict. The doctor, writing furiously in his note pad, said nothing.

"Ah ha a problem. Just as I thought." Corny mused. "Well," he said to himself, "if the Lord wants me to wait for Him in the ground until He comes that's ok too." But, if the truth be known, he definitely preferred the alternate route.

"Well, Mr. Krahn, I guess that about covers it," the doctor said rather nonchalantly.

'He guesses that about covers it? What does he mean he guesses. Isn't he taking this matter of life and death somewhat lightly?' Corny strained to keep the conversation light.

"So, I'll live a bit longer, will I doc?"

"Oh, I think quite a while longer if you take care of yourself. Take it easy on that rich Mennonite cooking. And don't start smoking," the doctor added with a laugh.

"I'm alright then?" Corny asked anxiously. "I don't need any medication or drugs?"

"Absolutely not. Your heart rate is good. Cholesterol results will be back next week. Don't expect a problem there. There's a slight enlargement of the prostate, but that's natural for a man your age."

Enlargement of the prostate is natural? Corny didn't know where the prostate was or what, if anything, it did. But it worried him nevertheless that it had grown and was perhaps this very moment getting bigger. "Shouldn't I be taking something for that? Some pills?" he asked the doctor.

"No, just watch your diet and make sure you get a little exercise," the doctor said as he opened the door to leave the examining room.

Corny rapidly came to the conclusion that this doctor couldn't be taken seriously. Entirely too casual, too nonchalant about such an important matter as a man's health, not to mention his very life. He decided then and there to make an appointment with another doctor.

Corny was puffing when he reached Dr. Cashman's third floor office in the four-storied Ketchum Building. It was Warden's tallest building but not high enough to warrant an elevator. Dr. Cashman will see you right away, Mr. Krahn," the secretary said with a patronizing smile —- the kind reserved for small children and old people.

The examination followed the same procedure as the previous one. The throbbing pulse as the cuff tightened its grip around the arm. The needle prick drawing a small tube of blackish blood. And later, in the examining room, the gloved hand probing the nether regions where Corny now knew the prostate resided.

"Taking any medication?" Dr. Cashman asked.

"Nothing." Corny had stopped taking his Edelkreuter since moving into town in anticipation of getting started on some real medicine from a doctor.

"How are you sleeping?" the doctor asked.

"Not as good as I used to when I was on the farm." He didn't mention the Edelkreuter, and how it had relaxed him before bedtime. Peering over his half moon glasses Dr. Cashman flipped open his note pad and ran his eyes from top to bottom and back again. "You're in pretty good shape for a man your age, Mr. Krahn, but I'll give you a prescription to fine-tune your blood pressure and we'll also try to bring the prostate down a bit."

"How about the sleeping?" Corny asked. "I'm starting to wake up about three every morning and can't seem to get back to sleep."

"Well, we can probably find something to remedy that too," the doctor said with a confident air.

"Now there," Corny said to himself as he walked back down the three flights of stairs," there is a real doctor. Knows what he's doing."

Before the year was out a few more problems surfaced. A tingling sensation in his left foot was diagnosed as poor circulation, and that pesky blood pressure was always on the rise. But, as Corny kept telling Tina, "there's a pill for every ill."

What he depended on most were the sleeping pills that helped him get a good night's rest and often a good afternoon's too. He was getting into the habit of taking more than the label called for. The extra doses helped him sleep sounder and longer, usually until noon.

By the second year of his retirement his prized Barbara Ann roses were going untended. The tools in his shop, each hanging precisely in its assigned place, remained untouched, and half a dozen ornamental lawn windmills he was making for friends and neighbours were lying around in various stages of completion. Activities that had once absorbed him for hours were no longer of interest. He even stopped reading *Der Botschafter.* If he had, he would have noticed an article that the Health Branch in Ottawa had pulled Edelkreuter off the market much to the consternation of the Winnipeg distributor, and the paper which had lost one of its best accounts. The article praised the enlightened Swiss, who made and exported the product, for their centuries-old knowledge of the healing powers of its various herbs. It chastised the Canadian medical establishment for its stubbornness in failing to recognize the merits of this time-tested folk medicine.

What the article didn't mention, and was of some concern to the authorities, was that the herbs constituted the smallest part of the potion. The other 90% would have comfortably held its own with anything produced by the most talented moonshiner in the Hills of Tennessee.

None of this no longer mattered to Corny who continued to take his "doctor" medicine religiously. His white capped prescription bottles were lined up on the kitchen counter like so many troops on parade. He slept much of the day and at mealtime picked away at Tina's cooking which he had once eaten with such relish. He constantly complained that the house was either too hot or too cold, and kept forgetting where he had left his glasses. These he now used only to read the Bible.

Even his Bible reading had changed. He avoided all comforting and uplifting parts, which Tina liked, and became obsessed with Revelations. He once told his wife that, like John, God was speaking to him in visions. "Only last night," he said, "I saw a woman in a purple and scarlet robe, wearing many precious stones. She was astride a red horse blaspheming God. In her hand she held a golden cup which she extended to me with her jewelled hand. With a crack of thunder an angel on a white charger appeared, unsheathed her sword, and knocked the cup from the woman's hand splintering it into a thousand pieces."

"You saw all this?" Tina asked incredulously.

"As sure as I'm seeing you right now. I should be writing all this down, but I'm always so tired." He then opened his well-worn Bible to the very last chapter of Revelations. "Dit es me wichtig," (this touches me deeply) he said to Tina in Low German as he began to read. "He who testifies to these things says, 'yes, I am coming quickly.' Amen. Come Lord Jesus."

Before the end of that month Tina was a widow. The minister comforted her by telling her that her man had gone to a better place. Her women friends patted her hand and clucked the prescribed condolences that, "it was God's will that he should go. Your husband is now with the Lord."

Tina was confused. Was Corny at this very moment in heaven with God? or would he have to wait in the ground until, in the words of the Negro spiritual, "that great gettin' up mornin'?" Why, she wondered to herself, hadn't she been given the gift of understanding the Bible the way Corny had. He may not have always been right, but he never had any doubts. He had always understood exactly what God's word taught on such matters as salvation, death and resurrection.

Tina worried, and she was lonely. Soon she began to feel poorly herself. She complained that she wasn't sleeping well, and that her nerves were bad. Her stomach was, what she called "touchy", insisting that the only food she could tolerate was Lipton's Cup-a-Soup, toast and tea.

She rarely turned on the radio, didn't bother getting the TV fixed, and restricted her reading of *Der Botschafter* to the obituary pages. One day she was leafing towards the obits when she realized she had picked up an old copy of the weekly. She was about to put it down when the word 'Edelkreuter' jumped from the page. She read the article and remembered there were still two cases in the basement which Corny had brought from the farm.

While her late husband had been a steadfast believer in doctoring, Tina harbored a deep and abiding suspicion of the medical arts. It was a skepticism that bordered on outright cynicism. She had never taken to Edelkreuter either the way Corny had but, she reasoned,if the doctors and druggists didn't want it sold it must have something going for it.

Tina put the paper down and began preparing her clothes for tomorrow's Sunday church service. She ran her fingers along the hangers, paused every so briefly at her favorite —- the burgundy silk dress she hadn't worn since Corny died. Her hand stopped at the black one, the one her husband liked. She brushed off the lint, which it seemed to attract like a magnet, laid it over a chair and got ready for bed.

It was ten o'clock, the time of day she dreaded most. Not that she had trouble falling asleep, but regular as the chiming of the Kröger clock in the hallway, she awoke in the wee hours of the morning and couldn't get back to sleep. As a result, she was tired most of the day.

'Ah, the Edelkreuter in the basement,' she thought to herself. On the farm Corny had found it most relaxing. She poured out half a tumblerful, and sipped slowly. She still didn't care for the taste, but yes, it did seem to calm her nerves. A comforting warmth enveloped her whole body. Well, for good measure, another half glass before bedtime wouldn't hurt.

In her dream she was leaning into a raging inferno and it was the intense heat on her face that woke her. The sun was already standing high, its narrow rays piercing the window pane with fire-striking power. She had overslept. More than overslept. It was ten past noon. She had missed church which would just now be getting out.

And it was so still. So eerily still. There were no cars churning up gravel on the road. No dogs barking. No cows mooing in neighboring pastures. Only a loose picket occasionally slapping against the garden fence whenever the lazy breeze picked up. She had been dressed for nearly an hour and still none of the usual neighborhood sounds. The Rempels hadn't driven by on their way home from church, and even allowing for visiting time in the foyer after the service, they should have been by half an hour ago.

A thought entered her mind. A strange thought. She dismissed it quickly, but it came right back. No, that simply wasn't possible. Then again, maybe it was. Had Jesus come in the night to take the saved, both living and dead, into his heavenly kingdom? Had she been left behind? For several minutes she sat almost paralyzed listening to the relentless ticking of the Kröger. Then, as if suddenly snapping to attention, she decided to go for a walk.

From her driveway she could look across the road directly onto the patio at the side of the Nickle house. Trocka Nickle, a big-bellied man in his late forties, was sitting with his feet up on a picnic table, a bottle of beer in one hand and a cigarette in the other. Tina didn't know, what the Mennonites called, his front name. He drove a transport so every one knew him as "trocka" Nickle. In any event, no big surprise that he hadn't been called. She ventured farther down the road to the Rempels, who had never missed church as long as she'd known them. The drapes were open. That was odd on such a hot day. She could see into the living room, but there was no sign of life. She walked along the side of the house and peered into the kitchen. Her heart nearly stopped. The scriptural calendar still showed Saturday. The Rempels hadn't torn off the Sunday morning sermonette. Perhaps they too had overslept and had to hurry to make it to church on time —- or?

Tina was in a state of near panic, half walking, half running, as she headed for Lydia Janzen's tiny house at the bend in the road. If Mennonites had believed in sainthood, Lydia would have been their first choice. She had been a missionary nurse in Mozambique all her adult life. When she turned seventy, after much prayer and meditation, the Lord led her into retirement. At home she taught adult Sunday School until her eyes gave out and her arthritis got really bad. The main door was open. Tina glanced through the closed screen door and knocked. There was no answer. Not a sound inside. She knocked harder and cocked her ear toward the door. Silence. She was about to leave when she heard the click of two wooden canes being grasped into one hand, and saw Lydia's stooped silhouette hobbling down the narrow hallway.

"Oh thank you dear Lord, thank you," Tina whispered tears welling up in her eyes. Lydia squinted at the door through thick milky glasses, pushing her face to within six inches of the screen. "Oh, it's you Tina. I guess I must have dozed off a bit. Please do come in."

"Well, I don't want to disturb you. Just taking a little walk. Thought I'd stop by to see if you're alright."

"You were probably worried because I wasn't in church this morning," Lydia said somewhat apologetically. Tina didn't reply. "I decided not to go," Lydia went on. "My arthuritis is acting up a bit, and I knew there would be no visiting after church because everybody would be rushing off to Squirrel Creek Park for the children's Sunday School picnic."

"Oh yes, the picnic. I'd forgotten," Tina whispered under her breath. She couldn't remember when she had been so happy. She listened enthralled to Lydia's stories about mission work in Africa even though she had heard them many times before. She even seemed to genuinely enjoy Lydia's rock-hard biscuits and weak tea.

There was an inexplicable light bounce to her every step as she walked home. Every breath she took was intoxicating. At her driveway she was welcomed by an assemblage of sparrows holding noisy court in the crab apple tree. And the Barbara Ann rose bushes.....hadn't been pruned in years and, look at them, loaded with buds. Tina walked to the unkempt garden behind the house. The strawberries were ripe and she hadn't even noticed. Well now, a batch of pyrushkis would definitely be on tomorrow's menu.

Before retiring, Tina prepared to read a passage from the Bible which she did every evening. But tonight she was in a particularly thankful mood, so she searched for something cheerful, something uplifting. Perhaps one of the nice psalms to end a splendid day. A most perfect day.

Everyone must walk in the light of his own heart's gospel

— T. Tanner

HONOURABLE MEN ALL

The brown manila envelope bearing the words "On His Majesty's Service" had been expected. It was early August 1941, a month since Ike had reported to the medical board and found to be fit for military service. His examination card had 1-A stamped on it.

He slowly pulled a table knife out of a kitchen drawer and took a long look at the address. 'Mr. Isaac P. Doerksen, Box 50, Kirkcaldy, Manitoba.' He carefully slit it open and began to read. 'Dear Mr. Doerksen:' (He had only been addressed as "Mr." once before when he'd been told to report for his medical). 'You are hereby summoned to appear before the Mobilization Board of Canada at the Court House in the town of Warden in the province of Manitoba on August 15, 1941 at 10:00 a.m. At that time your request for conscientious objector status will be heard before Mr. Justice John L. Stevenson. You are advised to appear before the board alone without counsel or any other person speaking on your behalf. Failure to appear ...' Ike folded the letter and slipped it back into the envelope.

"Warden on the 15th," he said to his mother, who was bent over a half submerged washboard in a tub full of work shirts. "Vy can dey us Mennonites not alone leave," she sighed.

Ike's mother was a slight, thin woman of 45. She had been through hard times. War, revolution and famine had etched their lines of march across her face. Perhaps as a reaction to the harsh hand fate had dealt her, her piety did not come naturally, seeming to serve as a veneer masking the bitterness of deep personal loss. Nevertheless she was a woman of simple faith. Above her shone the sun by day, and the moon and stars by night. Beyond them lay God's eternal heaven where a better life awaited her. The fires of hell, reserved for the souls of the damned, raged below. What might exist beyond her three-storied universe was not for her to know or ask.

She dried off her hands and hoisted a large basin of bread dough onto the table.

"In Holland four hundred years ago dey could us not alone leave. Also in Germany, then in Russia, and now in Canada dey can't us alone leave." As she spoke, she pushed first one fist then the other into a small mountain of white dough.

"You know Isaac, now it is nearly 150 years dat Tsarina Catherina our people to Russia brought from Germany." She paused ... with the grace of a wrestler throwing a compliant adversary she flipped the pillow-sized mound over and began kneading the other side.

"Ya, den dey said to our Mennonites, 'Ve vant farmers have. Soldiers need ve not.' De czar made it for us Mennonites in the First Var so they did not have anyone's life to take. Your fadder dey let as medic serve."

"If I had to," Ike interjected, "I'd join as a medic, but they say if they let all the Mennonite boys into the medical corps there wouldn't be room for anyone else."

His mother carried on as if she hadn't heard.

"Ya, your fadder carried no gun, and nobody did he ever kill. He stayed a good Mennonite. But de var took his life anyway."

"The cold and the snow. His lungs" Ike said, picking up the story he'd heard a hundred times. His father had loaded wounded soldiers on the Russian front onto horse drawn sleighs and wagons, and hauled them to the railway line where they were put on hospital trains. He was never well after that, and died ten years after that war ended.

"I guess the Russian generals never trusted us Mennonites because we're German," said Ike as a way of leading into the next story he'd also heard many times before.

"No, your fadder said sometimes dey vould let him not on the battle field, scared he over to Germans vould go."

"Lucky he didn't get captured. The Russians would have shot him after the war." Ike waited for his mother to pick up the story again.

"Ya, the Germans captured once a whole hospital train of Mennonite medics. 'Make it fast,' their Russian commander said, 'load dees vounded in tventy minuten and I give you all George Medal mit black and yellow ribbon.' De boys did it in fifteen minuten."

"Not fast enough," said Ike.

"No, not fast enough. Dey ver all prisoner taken. Ven dey ver to Germany sent, de Russians said dey spies and should be shot."

"But," Ike continued, "after they got home the Socialists came to power and saved their lives."

"You must before Judge Stevenson stand?" asked Ike's mother, abruptly changing the subject.

"Yes."

"Friesen's Harry vent before him - let him off."

"Yeh, ended up in a work camp in the B.C. bush for conscientious objectors," Ike said.

An endless tawny ocean of wheat, barley and oats, the monotony occasionally broken by green patches of late seeded crop, rolled past the train window. August had been a hot month, and the fields all seemed to be ripening at once. Ike wondered how his stepfather was making out on the south quarter which he had started cutting that morning.

"Even if you have to go, they'll give you a few months to help with the harvest", said Pete, as if reading Ike's mind. Pete Harms, who had his own appointment with Stevenson, had also boarded the train in Kirkcaldy.

Pete had a reputation for being a bit of a swell. In the eyes of the evangelical Mennonite faction to which Ike's mother and her second husband belonged, he was a 'worldly' chap. The evangelicals viewed him as a prime candidate to go to the front and get saved at one of their revival meetings.

Pete had a natural elegance which Ike secretly admired, and as a born again Christian felt guilty about it. His going to the Friday night movies at the Odd Fellows Hall and shooting pool at Gauthier's billiard rooms was certain to put a bit more grease on the skids leading Pete straight to the mouth of hell. Laughter came easily to Pete, and if he sensed that his immortal soul was in danger he didn't show it. He was always so sure of himself. He had been good in school, a smooth talker who knew all the angles. Even the "English" boys his age looked up to him. Except for being Mennonite, he was everything Ike was not.

"Hot isn't it," said Pete. Both boys had been silently staring out the window at the passing countryside for a long time. Ike had been trying to rub an arc of flyspecks off the window with his sleeve until he realized they were on the outside.

"Yeh, think I'll take off my jacket," said Ike, wishing he hadn't gone and got all dressed up in his scratchy blue serge suit ... just the pants, shirt and windbreaker, like Pete, would have been better.

He envied Pete's teal blue fedora too ... made him look just like the pictures of Clark Gable and Robert Taylor he'd seen in the movie magazines at the barber shop. Self consciously he pushed his salt and pepper cloth cap a bit farther under the small cardboard box tied with binder twine which held his safety razor, toothbrush and a pair of oversized boxer shorts his mother made on the old Singer sewing machine. His appearance before Judge Stevenson would require an overnight stay.

"I guess the Mennonite guys are in for a rough ride." Pete smiled, lighting up a tailor made Turret. "Kinda between the devil and the deep blue sea, like the English say. If we join up, we get kicked out of the church. That is if we've been baptized. I know some guys who didn't even volunteer; got called up, put on the khaki suit and now their families won't talk to them. Shunning it's called. Actually our Mennonites don't even have a word for it. They just seem to think it's what God wants them to do."

Pete paused to take a long drag on his cigarette sending two white shafts of smoke through his nostrils.

"If we tell old Mackenzie King where he can stick his draft notice he'll give us a couple of years at hard labour. If we're lucky we end up in some CO bush camp cutting trees nobody needs and building roads nobody drives on."

"I hear they might open up the Medical Corps for Mennonites," said Ike hopefully. "Like the czar did in Russia in the last war."

"Don't count on that either. Your old man's healthy. Your kid brother is fifteen and you've only got a half section."

"Can't figure it," said Ike. "Our neighbors, the McNaughtons got deferments for both their boys and they work the place with a tractor. Of course old man McNaughton's got a bad back."

"Yeh, " Pete sneered, "he's got a bad back and good connections. Guess we'll just have to go down in history as cowards. Cowards to the English if we don't fight, and cowards to our people if we do."

That word coward bothered Ike. He looked straight at Pete sitting in the seat opposite. He saw him not in his white shirt, suit pants and snappy felt hat cockily perched on his wavy blond head, but bare naked standing as if frozen on the river bank, muscular arms hanging limply at his sides.

It hadn't been more than three months ago, a Sunday ... one of those real scorchers that hit the prairies in early summer. It happened right after church.

It was a two mile hike in sweltering heat through thick bush to get to the Assiniboine, but Ike and Pete thought it was worth it. Both were annoyed when Helmut Wiebe insisted on tagging along. He was the same age as Ike and Pete, but slightly built and a poor swimmer.

But that wasn't why Helmut was an outcast among the Mennonite boys. Unlike other fathers, his did not farm. His, in fact, did very little of anything. Although he attended church, he didn't believe a word of it. The little money he earned by doing odd jobs went to buy tinned tobacco and strange books about stars and planets from a mail order house in the States. The family depended on charity and handouts.

The river was still running high after a heavier than usual spring run off. Two young Metis boys, their smooth brown skin glistening in the sun were already at the favored spot, so the three newcomers moved a bit farther up stream.

The shriek for help came just as Ike tossed his shorts over a nearby chokecherry bush. Pete was already at the river's edge testing the water with one foot. Helmut, slow as usual, was still in his pants. Pete was first on the scene. Ike was close behind, rubbing a shin he'd skinned tripping over a log. Both boys stopped abruptly on the high bank.

In the eddy below a mop of coal black hair billowed to the surface, sank, then rose again. One of the Metis boys, no more than ten, had dog paddled too close to a sharp drop off and got caught in the current. Pete, Ike and the other boy stood immobile as Helmut rushed past them. Still wearing his pants, he dove awkwardly into the spot where he'd seen a black circle of hair disappear under the water. An eternity of ten seconds passed before two heads bobbed out of the water. The boy had both arms locked around Helmut's scrawny red neck pulling him down so that only the top of his blond head showed. With one arm around the boy he made first one, then another desperate lunge at a partially submerged poplar which had been felled, then abandoned, by a beaver.

Ike and Pete watched motionless from the bank above as Helmut and the boy finally wrapped their arms around the fallen tree. Exhausted, they stayed in the water for a long time, resting their heads on the trunk. Slowly they made their way, monkey bar style, to the safety of the shore.

Without a word or a glance at Ike and Pete, Helmut put on his shoes, grabbed his shirt and disappeared into the bush headed for home.

"There's really no difference between a coward and a hero," said Pete staring blankly out the train window. "Both are motivated by fear."

'That Pete,' thought Ike, 'always reading those books about philosophy and stuff and being able to figure things out real good.' Yet, he wasn't convinced that Pete was right.

"Sometimes you can't slide a cigarette paper between what's right and what's wrong," Pete continued, lighting up another Turret.

"Yeh ... I hear a lot of Mennonites are buying or renting all the land they can get their hands on so their sons have a better chance of getting draft deferments for farm work."

"Nothing wrong with that," said Pete.

"Maybe not. Then there are all the guys getting themselves baptized in a real hurry so they can tell the judge they're church members."

"Like me," said Pete, blowing three perfect smoke rings against the window.

"Old Rev Schultz gave me the sprinkle job last Sunday. 'Course it's not so easy for you Brethren guys. You've got to get dunked."

"I wanted to get baptized this summer," Ike said. "My mother tried to arrange it, but the pastor from Winnipeg couldn't make it."

"Won't do you much good tomorrow."

"No, but I'd like to get baptized anyway, whether it helps with the draft board or not."

"Maybe you can squeeze it in before fall if you get harvest leave."

"Not likely. It's been so dry this summer Swanson's slough is nearly dried up and you can wade across the river where we swam in May."

"Warden, Warden, next stop Warden." the conductor sang out, steadying his ample frame on the wicker seat backs with one hand and fishing a gold watch out of his vest pocket with the other.

"If I can just persuade the judge I'm a CO, I'll be on easy street," Pete mused.

"Easy street?" asked Ike incredulously, "Easy street? What's easy about cutting trees in snow up to your armpits when it's forty below?"

Pete didn't answer. Then, almost as if he were talking to himself, he said, "Stevenson is tough. He chews nails and spits out ball bearings. If I show him my little baptismal certificate from old man Schultz it won't be worth shit."

"Easy Pete, no need to talk like that. We'll just tell the judge what's in our hearts. Whatever happens will be the Lord's will."

"Yeh, the Lord works in mysterious ways, doesn't he?" There was more than a tinge of sarcasm in Pete's voice.

Judge Stevenson took his powerful position on the War Services Board seriously. No, he took it more than seriously. He saw it as his God-given mission to get as many Mennonite men into uniform as possible and, while he was at it, free them from what he considered to be their misguided faith. In fairness to the judge, he was charged with the impossible task of plumbing the inner recesses of a man's conscience ... that unpredictable faculty that distinguishes bad from good, right from wrong.

That the Mennonite faith forbade the taking of human life, even in defence of one's country, was completely beyond the judge's comprehension. He himself had served with an infantry battalion in the First World War. As a university graduate he had automatically been given an officer's commission. After only a few months in England, and just before his unit set sail for France, Lieutenant John Stevenson returned to Winnipeg with his right foot in a cast. How he had been injured before reaching the front had remained something of a mystery.

Nevertheless, the judge had a reputation as a man with a keen sense of justice, and his new role as chairman of the local mobilization board gave him wide latitude in interpreting justice as he saw it. In hearing the petitions of conscientious objector applicants, like Ike and Pete, he was not only judge but also prosecutor and jury. Each candidate appearing before him, no matter how inarticulate, was obliged to act in his own defence.

Pete wasn't inarticulate. He had, as both his friends and

detractors said, a way with words. There were even those who suggested he'd be a natural as a preacher. Pete thought his talents could be put to better, and more lucrative, use as a criminal defence lawyer. But his father scratched out a precarious living for his large family on a quarter section hard scrabble farm. So, as soon as Pete finished the eleventh grade he went to work as a farm hand. His dream of getting his Twelve and going on to law school remained just that - a dream.

Nor was there any encouragement from his parents, or the rest of the Mennonite community. Higher education was a sure fire way of being led from the straight and narrow. The legal profession in particular was frowned upon. Courts of law were decidedly un-Christian and the swearing of oaths contrary to the Bible.

None of this mattered in the least to Pete. The only doctrine of Mennonite faith that had any significance in his life, since getting his draft notice, was that of non-resistance. The task at hand was convincing the judge of his sincerity.

"We're both still up for tomorrow morning," Pete said, as he scanned the list posted on the door. "Gives us the rest of the day to listen to more of Wayne's b.s."

"He's not such a bad guy, Pete. He helped me write out my opening statement for the judge. I think that's what he called it, an opening statement."

"You mean he wrote it for you. Typed it out too. I don't think that was too smart. Like you said Ike, you should just say what's in your heart."

"When I get up there I won't be able to say two words straight. I know what I want to say, but my mind will be a blank and I'll make a fool of myself."

Wayne Ketchum was, what the Kirkcaldy folks would call, a city slicker. His father, a prominent Winnipeg lawyer, had grown up in Warden where his older brother still operated the family hotel. Wayne worked for his uncle behind the desk during the summer when he wasn't at university. His self-assured manner and neat appearance impressed Ike. His short-cropped hair seemed to be molded on his head, every single strand of which knew its assigned place. There was no rooster tail at the back that had to be constantly tamed with Brilliantine. His complexion was astonishingly clear without even the hint of a blemish. No pitch fork had ever raised a callous on his long, narrow hands.

"Well Pete, guess your friend should be getting acquainted with the judge about now," said Wayne. "My old man knows Stevenson," he went on, with the emphasis on knows. "He's in thick with the Liberals in Ottawa. The old man says your bishops are doing a lot of complaining and the politicians are starting to listen."

"You'd think that with all the trouble Mackenzie King's having with the Frenchies he'd be happy as the proverbial pig with Stevenson slapping us into uniform." said Pete.

"Sure, that's what Stevenson thinks. But Mennonites vote too. Winning elections is just as important to King as winning the war. Maybe more important," Wayne added with a laugh.

"Yep," Wayne continued, "Stevenson wanted to get into Parliament in the worst way. But every time he tried, some Tory rattled a little skeleton in his closet and he withdrew."

"What do you mean, a skeleton?"

Wayne lowered his voice to a near whisper. "It's just a rumour. But the story goes that Stevenson injured himself on purpose in the last war while he was training in England. Broke every little bone in one foot with a trenching tool. Says it was an accident. Who's to tell? There was nobody around at the time. But it got him out of the army and back home."

The judge was much smaller than Ike had imagined. He was impeccably dressed. The creases on the trousers of his dark gray suit were sharp as a butcher's knife.

Ike was conscious of how rounded his were, but realized it was the best his mother could do with the heavy irons she had to heat on the wood burning kitchen stove. And the judge's shirt - it was so crisp and white. Ike's eyes were drawn to the judge's polished black shoes as he strode to his seat on the raised dais at the front of the court room. He thought he noticed a slight, almost imperceptible limp every time he put weight on his right foot.

"Mr. Isaac Doerksen?" the clerk looked inquiringly at Ike. "You are up first. Remember to address Judge Stevenson as 'Your Honor'".

Ike stood before the judge the same way he stood in church during prayers, his arms hanging down, hands folded over his fly. After intently studying some papers for a long time, Judge Stevenson slowly raised his eyes over his reading glasses and fixed his gaze on Ike. For some time he said nothing. Then ...

"Why don't you like your country, Mr. Doerksen?" Ike was taken aback. When he opened his mouth he was surprised to hear himself speaking in the upper register of his throat.

"I, I don't like ... I mean I do like my country," Ike stammered. Then quickly added the 'Your Honor'".

"Speak up young man. Don't mumble. You like your country, but not enough to fight for it, is that what you are saying?" The judge didn't wait for a reply. "You know, Mr. Doerksen, if you do not help your country in her hour of need you are helping Hitler. Is that what you want to do?"

"Nnno, Your Honor."

"Then why don't you want to serve in the military?"

"My mother ... uh, I mean my parents. They say it is wrong to kill."

"Don't any of you young men think for yourselves? Every last one of you comes in here whining about what your parents or your preachers told you to say. And these are the same parents who only a few years ago were begging to be let into this great country because the Communists were taking their land away and starving them. Is this the thanks you give your new country?"

Ike sensed that the judge had already made up his mind and his conclusions were not in his favour.

'I just hope he doesn't ask me whether I'm a member of the church,' Ike thought, 'and have to explain about my mother not being able to get the preacher out before Swanson's slough got all weedy, and the river nearly dried up.' But he didn't ask. He assumed.

"I get you fellows in here all the time. Get themselves baptized just in time for these hearings and think that will get them off. Well young man that kind of a dodge doesn't cut any ice with me."

Again, the judge didn't seem to expect a response. He immediately posed another question.

"Mr. Doerksen, why should I exempt you from military service by granting you conscientious objector status?" This time he obviously did want an answer. Ike fumbled a folded piece of paper out of his hip pocket and began reading: "I, Isaac P. Doerksen, of Kirkcaldy, Manitoba hereby claim conscientious objector status on religious and mor...." Judge Stevenson whipped off his glasses and fairly bellowed.

"What in God's name are you doing?"

"I don't speak so good Your Honor. I got it all written out for you."

"Give me that!"

The judge grabbed his glasses again and began scanning the neatly typed page. He flipped it over to look at the other side, which was blank, and dropped it on the table as if he had accidentally picked up something with a bad smell.

"Are you trying to make a fool out of me?" he roared, removing his glasses very slowly.

"N...no, Your Honor."

"Well then, perhaps you'll tell me who wrote this for you."

"A ... a friend." Ike didn't want to implicate Wayne even though he was only a casual acquaintance. "A friend," Ike continued, "he helped put my thoughts on paper."

"You were clearly instructed before appearing at this hearing not to employ counsel or get assistance of any kind. You are obviously a young man who has never learned to follow orders. Well, we can correct that. Conscientious objector status is denied. You will receive official notification and details by mail."

"B...but Your Honor," Ike interjected lamely.

Judge Stevenson's voice was tight and hard. "I have nothing further to say to cowards."

The hearing had lasted less than ten minutes. But in that short time something had changed in Ike. He somehow didn't feel like the same person who had walked into the courthouse. What exactly had gone out of his life that morning, or what had come into it, he couldn't say. But he felt different. The clarity and openness with which he had viewed the world up to that moment had suddenly become dark and murky.

"Didn't go so good, eh?" Wayne asked, as he glanced up from behind the reception desk.

"Nope."

"You mean my little presentation didn't impress the judge?"

"Guess not. Maybe too many therefores and whereases." Ike

slumped into a large leather armchair, resting his head on its high back. His eyes wandered across the lobby ceiling, walls and doors without registering what they were seeing. "Coward." The word had stung, and it still stung.

Ike's mind was a swirl of contradictions. His mother never let him forget that this wonderful country had taken them in as refugees from Stalin's terror when no other country wanted them. Was he now failing his country in her hour of need as the judge had charged? Or, was his mother right, that such gratitude did not demand killing people or offering sons as cannon fodder? And she knew all about cannon fodder from Ike's father who had spent two years gathering shattered bodies and parts of bodies from the battlefields of Tannenburg and Ostrolenka. And to what end?

Then there was the all important article of Mennonite faith ... non-resistance. Failure to live up to that admonition could bring another into play ... shunning. Was Ike ready or capable of cutting his emotional and religious ties to family, church and community and face a cold and indifferent outside world of which he knew so little? If he refused military service, as his faith demanded, was he prepared to spend a year or more in jail at hard labour as the law demanded?

"So what are you going to do?" The words came from Wayne sitting behind his desk preparing next week's beer order.

"Don't know," said Ike, continuing to stare at the wall in front of him. "Wouldn't mind getting into the medical corps. My dad was a medic in the last war. Russian army. Never carried a gun. Never fired a shot. Pete says I don't stand a chance."

"Probably not." Medical's full. It's infantry they want," said Wayne.

"Well, I'm not about to go over there and kill people," Ike said defiantly. "But," he added with quick defensiveness, "I'm no coward."

There was silence. Ike had expected Wayne to say something like 'of course you're not', but Wayne said nothing.

"What are you going to do?" Ike asked, unable to hide his anger. "You're draft age."

"Me? I'm already in. Sort of. Second looey in the university contingent."

"What?" Ike had no idea what he was talking about.

"Second Lieutenant. Army's university unit. They make all us brainy types officers right off the bat," Wayne laughed. A girlish laugh Ike thought. "I'll be going active as soon as I get my law degree this fall."

"Infantry?" Ike asked.

"Heck no, the old man's got it all worked out ... Vancouver, if you can believe it. The Army's Judge Advocate General's Department."

"What's that?"

"Army lawyer Ike, I'm going to be an army lawyer. Help guys like you get your ass out of a sling when you get into trouble ... or get it into one. Depends which side they put me on."

After the typed statement to the judge, Ike wasn't sure he'd ever want any help from Wayne. He pulled his Westclox watch out of a side pocket of his dress pants and checked the time. Pete should be out of the hearing soon.

'Why couldn't his parents be more like Pete's,' he thought. Pete's folks were easy going. They weren't dogmatic church goers, and if Pete ended up in the army which, given his own experience, he was sure he would, his parents wouldn't lose a minute's sleep over it.

"Guess your folks will give you a pretty rough time when they see their Johnny come marching home with shiny buttons on his suit, eh, Ike?" Wayne said somewhat sarcastically. Ike didn't answer.

"Tell you what you do."

'Here he goes again,' Ike thought, 'more of Wayne's half-baked advice.'

"Your mother .. er your folks, would tolerate you being a medic ... no blood on your hands ... well you know what I mean," Wayne chuckled.

"Yes, they would," Ike replied hopefully.

"Here's what you do. Sure as God made little green apples they'll whip you into infantry after basic. Unless of course you decide to go to jail which I don't think you will. So, just go to the base tailor, or better still slip the corporal in Quarter Master's a few bucks and get yourself a set of medic's shoulder flashes. For good measure get a sew-on Red Cross badge too. That should look good in church. Sew them on your tunic when you're on leave, and presto!, you're a medic. Until you get back to base of course."

"I don't know," Ike said, after giving Wayne's latest scheme some thought. "Sounds dishonest to me. Maybe even illegal." Wayne was clearly annoyed that Ike hadn't responded with more gratitude.

"You naive Mennonite sod busters better learn something. Your sheltered little world of loving thy neighbour, turning the other cheek, and all that bullshit won't get you very far in the real world. I'm afraid you're in for a few bruising surprises."

Wayne snapped a piece of paper into his typewriter and went on tapping out his beer order. Ike remained silent, his eyes scanning the by now familiar walls of the hotel lobby. There were the portraits of King George VI and Queen Elizabeth. The King was dressed in a scarlet military tunic, his chest draped with medals. The Queen wore a snow white gown, a blue sash hung across her ample bosom. Under the portraits was a crudely lettered banner, "For King and Country." Ike was studying the stuffed head of a bull buffalo directly above the door bearing the sign 'LICENSED PREMISES" when it swung open. It was Pete coming in from the street through the beer parlor entrance, a mile-wide grin stretched across his face.

"So what have you got to be so happy about. Don't tell me you got a deferment?" Ike asked.

"Deferment hell. I got full conscientious objector status." Pete was still grinning from ear to ear. Ike stood dumfounded. He had always thought he had a stronger case than Pete. Sure, Pete had got himself baptized but it wasn't his fault the Mennonite Brethren insisted on baptism by full immersion and Pete's church just sprinkled. And it wasn't his fault the preacher couldn't come from Winnipeg sooner, and that Swanson's slough had turned into mud.

'Well,' he thought, 'maybe none of it would have mattered. The judge seemed to have made up his mind the minute he laid eyes on him, and Wayne's stupid statement probably clinched it.'

'But,' Ike reasoned, 'the judge could have gotten Pete real easy on a technicality. He hadn't filed his claim for CO status within the required eight days after getting his letter to report for his medical.'

"Yeh," Pete exuded, with a faint whiff of beer on his breath, "the good Lord sure does work in mysterious ways."

"How did you do it?" Ike asked incredulously.

"Piece of cake old pal - - - a piece of cake. Oh sure, the guy climbed up one side of me and down the other for filing late, but my father - - - I didn't call him the old man, - - - thought father would sound more respectful, so I says my father was sick and I had to help him out on the farm and couldn't get to the post office."

Ike knew that was a lie. When Pete's dad was sick, and often when he wasn't, it was his mother who did the work.

"As for my baptism, I told him it just worked out that way. The public profession of my faith as a Christian and a Mennonite is something very close to my heart." The Reverend Ellsworth Carlson, the evangelist on the Fargo radio station, couldn't have said it with more conviction.

Pete was momentarily preoccupied with backhanding a blue cloud of cigarette smoke when Ike jumped in.

"Guess he must have believed you."

"Not a word," Pete replied matter of factly.

"Then how come he let you off?"

"Well," Pete continued, "I told him about how I was going to bugger up my hand by sticking it in the grain crusher drive belt - - - about how I'd heard that if you injure yourself bad enough the army won't take you. But, I told him I decided not to because that wouldn't be an honourable thing to do, and if I ever did such a thing I wouldn't be able to look at myself in the mirror." That stupid grin spread over Pete's face again.

"Well, I tell you the old judge's false choppers nearly fell out of his mouth. He looked down at his papers for a long time, took off his glasses but didn't look up. Then he said, 'Mr. Harms, you have made a most convincing case concerning your request for conscientious objector status. You are an honourable man. We are honourable men all. It gets down to a matter of con-science doesn't it ?' Then he says, 'on behalf of His Majesty's government my request for CO status is granted.' End of story."

"I don't know why you're so happy Pete. Dragging logs out of the bush in Ontario or busting rock in B.C. isn't what I'd call a holiday."

"Ike, old pal, none of that crap for me. You know the big red brick building up on the hill in Brandon?:

"You mean the Mental?"

"I mean the Provincial Psychiatric Hospital. I'm checking in." Pete roared with laughter. Ike was indeed wondering whether his friend had lost his mind.

"Yeh," Pete went on, "they're taking COs at the hospital as male nurses. Already got a line on an opening."

"You're crazy Pete," said Wayne who had been silently listening with undisguised amazement. "Who in their right mind would want to clean up after a bunch of loonies who've forgotten how to go to the toilet?"

"Just think of the side benefits old pal." The 'old pal' was beginning to grate on Ike's nerves.

"Side benefits?" Ike asked.

"Right. There must be a hundred female nurses up there. Husbands and boyfriends overseas. You know what I mean?" Pete gave Ike an exaggerated wink and a jab in the ribs as he walked towards the check out desk. Matter of factly, and without looking at Ike, Pete said in a low voice, - "I ran into Helmut's old man on the way back from the court house."

"Oh, what's Helmut up to?"

"He's in jail."

"Helmut's in jail? Helmut? What did he do?"

"Nothing. Well, I guess Stevenson wouldn't think so. Called Helmut a few nasty names and turned him down for conscientious objector status. Didn't show for military training and got himself tossed in the jug. Twelve months hard labour."

Ike spoke with undisguised bitterness. "Well, at least us Mennonite farm boys know all about hard labour."

"It's not the hard labour that will get to him," said Wayne. "It's the older prisoners and even some of the guards."

"They give the kids a bit of a hard time, do they? Pete inquired with a mocking laugh.

"Yeh, you might say that, if you know what I mean," Wayne muttered under his breath. "You know some of those guys prefer you pretty boy hicks over the ladies." There was a look of annoyance on Pete's face. He fancied himself as something of a man of the world and certainly didn't consider himself a hick.

"See what you've got to look forward to?" said Pete, as if he was already distancing himself from Ike's mundane little world.

Ike never did cotton on to what all the sniggering about pretty boys had been about, but he knew that Wayne was right on at least one count. Growing up in the comforting cocoon of a Mennonite community was to be made vulnerable to all kinds of unsuspected hurts and truths. He'd have to brace himself against the chill winds of a hostile outside world he instinctively knew was waiting for him.

Pete snapped the brim of his fedora with his index finger, and pushed it ever so slightly into the fashionable rakish angle. "Don't take all that guff about buggery in jail too seriously," he told Ike who was tightening the binder twine around his cardboard packing box.

"Don't you worry. I won't be putting on no jail bird's suit. Next time you see me in Kirkcaldy, I'll be all decked out in the King's uniform with RCAMC - - - Royal Canadian Army Medical Corps flashes on my shoulders, and a red cross sewn on my sleeve. Everybody will be happy, Judge Stevenson, the prime minister, our English neighbors, the Mennonite church and my parents. At least they'll be as happy as they ever get."

"You're dreaming Ike. Our preachers have run up against a stone wall in Ottawa trying to get a special Mennonite medic unit."

"Well, let's just say that the Lord truly does work in mysterious ways."

He will baptize you with the holy spirit and fire

— Matthew 3:11

DRINK OF THAT CUP

That Ike would become a minister had always been assumed...at least by his mother. At birth she saw him not as an infant in need of diapering, but as a tall, handsome young man standing behind a pulpit preaching the Gospel. This, her first born, was to be her gift to God.

There would be two winters of Bible School in Altbach and, if there was money, a year or so at the Mennonite College in Hillsboro, Kansas. Then a few more years practicing on the tiny congregation at Kirkcaldy, while continuing to work on the farm, before taking on one of the large Mennonite Brethren churches in Winnipeg. Not that Ike's mother approved of the big city churches. They were getting entirely too worldly with those highly varnished plush-seated pews. And just think of it, choirs wearing gowns and some of the girls with makeup.

It would be up to her son to shepherd these wayward flocks back to the simple, pious faith of their fathers before matters got entirely out of hand.

But, there was no time to be lost. The war had set her plans back. Those years could be made up, of course, but now Ike himself was her main concern.

She shared her anxiety with Ike's stepfather, lamenting that her oldest son just wasn't the same boy since he'd come home from the war. She complained that he was spending too much time with that no-good Peter Harms; that he was missing too many family prayers and that when he did pray with the rest of the family, his heart didn't seem to be in it. If only she could get Reverend Fast to come out from Winnipeg to have a talk with him.

Reverend Fast was a bit too modern for her liking too, but he was one of those painfully friendly Mennonite preachers who tried to talk to young people on their own level. Because of this, he was much in demand at the city churches, and rarely ventured into backwaters like Kirkcaldy. Sometimes, Ike's mother ruminated, when a Christian comes back to the church after having been out in the cold world for a long time he needs a spiritual warming up. Perhaps in Ike's case a more formal rededication of faith was called for. That he might be an out and out backslider she simply refused to contemplate.

This whole army business annoyed her. No, it made her angry. Why did Ike have to get himself talked into the service when Loewens' Abe, Baergs' Jake, and even Wiebes' Helmut (after doing his time in jail) were all allowed to do essential farm labour? And Friesens' Harry was released early from CO work in the B.C. bush. Even Harms' Pete, that good for nothing, had been back for months from alternative service at the 'Mental'. And why did Ike have to let himself be pushed into overseas duty? As a draftee he could have done his service right here in Canada.

Now here it was, the war in Europe over for four months and Ike just home. And then there was that gossipy Elsie Ratzlaff spreading rumours that Ike hadn't really been in the medical corps to begin with. Now if Ike's mother knew one thing, it was that her son had been a medic just like his father in the last war. It had said so right on his uniform. There was even a red cross sewn on his sleeve.

Well, that pluida zak got hers but good. At the next meeting of the sewing circle Ike's mother not only ignored Elsie, but also her famous peppermint cookies. And when they were passed around she wouldn't deign to even glance down at the plate.

At least Ike had agreed to one thing. He'd get himself baptized.

"Doerksen, you might as well get yourself water-proofed with the rest of these unwashed heathens." It was the voice of the company sergeant. Ike gave him a quick smile and shook his head. Without a stir the line of men, who'd been drinking and carousing the night before, moved toward a table set up in an open English field. On a snow white cloth stood a silver pitcher, bowl and goblets. The men silently approached the robed chaplain who sprinkled water on each head. Just as quietly they moved to kneel in the tall grass waiting to receive their first and, for some, their last communion.

As the line shortened, Ike edged closer to Merv Feldman who had also declined the sergeant's invitation.

"The morality squad is working overtime now that it's showtime," Merv quipped. He liked Merv. He came from Winnipeg's ethnic North End, and didn't need a long explanation of what a Mennonite was. He was A Company's joker - a wiseacre the sergeant called him.

But it always seemed to Ike that Merv's endless store of one-liners was a cover for a nagging suspicion that he wasn't really accepted as one of the boys. It was a feeling Ike shared.

"You and I are a lot alike", he told Ike one day during one of his rare serious moments. "Sure we're on opposite sides of the religious fence and all that, but we're both a 'people apart'. The only difference is that some day your kids and their kids will blend in with the crowd. Mine won't, and I won't want them to. Once a Jew, always a Jew."

The line was down to two. "If you're going to go, you'd better go now." Merv whispered. "What makes you think I want to go?" Ike replied testily.

"Never know, maybe the chaplain can bullet proof you too."

"Don't joke about this. Maybe it doesn't mean beans to you, but it has meaning for me." With that, Ike wheeled and walked toward the table.

In the name of the Father
Of the Son
and the Holy Ghost

The cow paths Ike and his friends had used to get to the river a life time ago were now a sandy two-rutted trail. In dry weather it could safely accommodate cars. On this sunlit Sunday, fifteen vehicles formed a caravan that slowly wound its way down to the river. At the river side the congregation sang.

Ich weiss einen Strom
dessen herrliche Flut
Fliesst wunderbar stille durch's land

"A real Mennonite baptism. Full immersion," Ike thought. "Not some pipe-sucking Anglican chaplain dribbling a few drops of water on your hair." And yet -

A tranquil, peaceful day under the palest of blue English skies. Serenity washed over him like a warm wave when the chaplain put his hand on his head. Like an orgastic release the unbearable tension, the jangling nerves, that sickness of soul which had rendered him a virtual wreck for weeks miraculously evaporated.

That the Royal Winnipeg Rifles would be part of the Allied assault on Europe was known. That they would be part of the first wave to hit the beaches somewhere in Normandy was quietly assumed.

"Careful Reverend, there's a sharp drop off to the right here," Ike warned as he and the preacher waded into the water. They were near the spot where the Metis boy had nearly drowned.

"You can't beat being baptized in a river," the minister said in hushed tones as they pushed their legs against the massaging current. "Our churches in the cities are installing baptismal tanks. There's nothing wrong with that, but a river is still best. Our Lord was baptized in a river." They stopped chest deep in water.

The cold seawater hit Ike like a kick in the groin, yet he welcomed it. Seconds before, the landing craft's ramp had dropped with a shuddering thud. Thank God. Free. Free at long last from the stench of vomit; the writhing wounded. Down. Down. Water over his ammunition pouches, running into his collar. Now lapping at his mouth. Dear God, didn't I put enough air into the life belt? They say drowning's rather pleasant. So somebody's drowned and lived to tell about it? These crazy thoughts flashed through Ike's mind in micro seconds just as his toes bumped against a solid bank of sand.

Like a man in a bad dream trying to flee danger, only to find that his legs won't move, Ike desperately lunged against the waves with every ounce of strength he could muster. Straining his arms to keep his rifle above water he could see, through eyes half blinded by saltwater, spits of fire coming from machine gun turrets on high concrete breakwaters. A man beside him flailed his arms in the pink foam, dragging a pair of mangled legs behind him.

The horrible beauty of the countryside. Camouflaged death crouching behind early summer's pea-green hedgerows. Cold contempt for the pale upturned teutonic faces. All mercy drained from men's souls. No thought projected beyond this day...this precious God-given day, heralded by a crowing rooster in yet one more stinking French farmyard. This the most perfect of communions. The communion of men in battle.

This is my body which is given to you,
do this in remembrance of me...
let a man examine himself
and so let him eat of that bread
and drink of that cup, for he who eats and drinks
unworthily eats and drinks
damnation unto himself

The little country church was packed for Ike's baptismal communion. Pete, now selling insurance and trying to get into law school, was there. He smirked whenever he caught Ike's eye. Helmut had driven up with his wife all the way from North Dakota where he had his own church. Ike fidgeted uncomfortably on a front pew, embarrassed that recently baptized teenagers were among those passing judgment on his suitability for church membership. He remembered them as awkward, pimply-faced adolescents.

The Reverend spoke. "Brothers and sisters, it is my God-given privilege to welcome into your fellowship here in Kirkcaldy, Brother Isaac Doerksen." In his testimony Isaac quoted Paul. 'Brethren I have lived my life with a perfectly good conscience before God up to this day.' It is my prayer that these words apply to each and every one of us.

"I know that Isaac's parents, this church...and yes God, have great plans for him. We pray that like Paul, he will be a witness in a sinful world, and honestly serve the God of our forefathers."

Try as he might, Ike could not muster even a pretense of the joy beaming in his mother's face. There wasn't so much as a hint of the transcendent peace and tranquility of that very special day in that memorable English meadow. Had it all been merely the catalyst that triggered a release of pent up nerves and anxiety of the horror that lay ahead? Or had it been a truly life defining mystical moment upon which he should have built his own convictions and beliefs? Of all the people Ike could have talked to about his depressed state, he chose Pete.

"Don't let them talk you into being some Bible thumping bush preacher Ike. You'll spend the rest of your life sniffing out doubts, then going through all kinds of theological contortions trying to exorcise them. Why do we Mennonites believe, or at least pretend to believe? It's so we'll be found acceptable by the other believers, that's why."

"Maybe we can't take everything in the Bible literally like Mennonites are supposed to," Ike ventured, "but you can't argue with Christ's teachings. I'm on solid ground there."

"Listen to me, Ike. You're young. Been places. Done things most men don't even dream about. You're going to get veterans' allowance. Why not go to university. Grow. For God's sake, get some fun out of life."

"I don't want to hurt my mother anymore than I already have," Ike replied.

"So you're going to go through life hurting yourself instead, worrying whether you're really saved or not. You're going to twist your mind all up with that "End Times" guff, some deranged prophet writing about beasts with ten horns and seven heads rising out of the sea. There's more to life than that."

The next morning found Ike standing in front of the mail drop at the post office. For a brief moment he looked at the address on the envelope.

The Registrar,
Altbach Bible School,
Altbach, Man.

He pushed it part way into the slot, held it for a second, then let it drop.

It is important to have the strength of our convictions – and our doubts

— Eric Sevareid

SOMETHING OF VALUE

Ike awoke with a vague, uneasy feeling. In his sleep a disembodied voice, like a grand inquisitor, had peppered him with questions: "who, how, why?" He had been unable to come up with answers, and now, only seconds later, he couldn't even remember the questions that were so clear in his dream. But the voice, the heavy German accented voice had been none other than that of Dr. Heinemann his biblical languages teacher.

He glanced at his watch. It was ten past eight. He'd missed breakfast even though it was served an hour later on Saturdays.

The year at Altbach Bible School was drawing to a close, and it had not been a good one for Ike. Intellect seemed to hold no place in the classroom or in extra curricular activities. If reason ever raised its head among the student body it was, Ike sensed, immediately put to work dousing the doubts it had spawned. Ike could not dispel his own doubts that had been nibbling at the perimeters of his faith almost from the first day at Altbach. Somehow, somewhere, he didn't know where or when, he had been infected by intellectual thought and imagination, twin intruders refusing to co-exist with church theology. He had tried, oh, how he had tried, to suffocate them at birth; to submerge them in a faith that viewed questioning as a character flaw, if not an outright sin.

Students were expected to, and did, swallow biblical truths blindly. Discussion, what there was of it, was carefully channeled to ensure a safe arrival at a predetermined destination. No one dared follow his thoughts wherever they might lead. The opening address by the school's principal had dealt with the matter of education as he, and by implication the entire teaching staff, defined it.

> *Education means to love our Mennonite culture, nurture programs in training children, emphasize freedom of conscience and academics but, in keeping with the work of Christ crucified and risen, and not departing from the principles of faith and life of our parental homes.*

"Emphasizing freedom of conscience and academics, but......."
Ike suppressed a chuckle when he heard those words. They
reminded him of his first day of basic training in the army.

"You spoiled bunch of momma's boys are free to do whatever
the hell you want," the Sergeant bellowed. Then spreading a
grin across his face, and lowering his voice to a murmur added,
"as long as you do exactly as I tell you. Do we all understand
each other?"

"So, why not just play the old army game?" Ike asked himself.
"Keep your nose clean, let others do the thinking, and get out
at the first opportunity."

Liberally sprinkling scriptural quotes in every assignment,
preferably from the New Testament, seemed to satisfy the
teachers. Talking about foreign missions? There's the old
standby, "Go ye into all the world and preach the gospel to
every creature....." Writing about steadfastness? Lots of supporting material there. ".....Jesus the author and finisher of our
faith..." Even the dullest student could simply open the Bible
and the quotes came tumbling out like trite predictions from
fortune cookies.

Ike hated himself for thinking that way. It was sacrilegious.
And, if anyone else in school had similar thoughts, they weren't
letting on. Maybe, Ike thought, his roommate, who in unguard-
ed moments let the odd damn or bloody slip into his conversation, was wrestling with the demons of doubt too.

Menno Toews had been at work on an assignment for hours
before Ike finally dragged himself out of bed.

"What ya working on?" Ike yawned.

"Poetical Books of the Old Testament," Menno replied, matter
of factly.

"Practical books of the Old Testament? I thought they were
all practical."

"I didn't say practical, I said poetical. It's one of our courses
in Third Year."

"They must trust you guys in Third to handle that stuff."

"What do you mean by `that stuff? Our doctrine of faith says
both the Old and New Testament are divine revelation, verbally
inspired by the Holy Spirit."

"I know, I know," Ike replied. "But you're into biblical poetry,
and I guess that includes the Songs of Solomon, doesn't it?"

121

"Sure does," there was a tone of authority and certainty in Menno's voice.

"Well, no disrespect," Ike countered, "but don't you think old Solomon was a bit of a frisky fellow describing his lovely lady as a palm tree with breasts like coconut clusters? But then, I guess he just wrote what God wanted him to write."

Menno wasn't amused. "You miss the point. Maybe when you've been at this as long as I have," he sneered, "you'll understand that these are simply allegories of what was to come, the bond between Christ and his Church revealed to us later in the New Testament."

Menno put down his pen and took off his thickish glasses. During the entire time he'd been talking to Ike, he hadn't looked up once. Now he leaned forward in his chair and looked at Ike, like a father about to set an errant child straight.

"You know Ike, I'm reminded of what Henry Bergen, who used to teach Life of Christ in First Year, told us on our very first day. He said that the teachers are there to give us an education and God is in the classroom to give us the inspiration. But if you ain't got common horse sense, neither God nor the teachers can teach you a da, er darn thing."

'That's my problem, nothing makes sense.' Ike didn't dare verbalize the thought. He stretched out to his full six feet, two inches on his freshly made bed, cupping his hands behind his head. He glanced up at the wall clock and sat up with a start. The Winnipeg bus would be leaving in forty-five minutes. He tossed his razor and a clean shirt into a small khaki kit bag he'd kept after his discharge. Almost as an after thought he added a book to read on the bus, *Living In Christ*, sub-titled, *guidelines for today's Christian.*

"So, you're off to the bright lights again," Menno said with poorly disguised sarcasm.

"Yeh, few people I haven't seen in a while, like Merv Feldman, an old army buddy."

"Feldman. Related to Isadore Feldman the communist Winnipeg alderman?"

"Merv's dad."

"Ike, I'm worried about you. It's bad enough being friendly with non-Christians here in town. Now you're socializing with the Winnipeg communists."

"It's not like that. You know as well as I do that I've got no use for communists after what they did to our people in Russia. But Merv's no communist. He and I go back a ways. Been in some tight spots together. There are things I can't talk about to anyone but Merv."

"Why not try talking to Jesus, and your fellow born again brothers? You know, our Men's Christian Fellowship meets tonight. Billy Joe Garner from the Moody Bible Institute in Chicago is in town. He'll be dropping by."

"Already heard him. He spoke to our First Year class on, `Jesus, the Founder of Modern Business'."

"Sounds like the kind of message all of us who will be witnessing in the business world could use," Menno said. His plan was to join his father in the family hardware business after graduation.

"Yeh, Billy Joe told us that if Jesus was living today, he'd probably be a national ad executive instead of a carpenter." Menno frowned. "Did he give you a biblical basis for that view?"

"Yeh, said Jesus had the smarts, that was his word, the smarts, to see the business potential of twelve ordinary men, and forge them into a public relations organization that hasn't been equalled since."

Menno banged a fist into an open hand. "Now that's the kind of Christian fire power we could do with more of around here. Too bad we can't get some thunder like that into old milktoast Heine."

"You won't find a better teacher of Hebrew and Greek," Ike said. Menno stood by his opinion. "Sure, he knows his stuff alright. But, well, he's just not very spiritual, if you know what I mean. Haven't you noticed that he's all Greek syntax, and no sin and salvation?" Ike suspected that the real reason Menno didn't like Dr. Heinemann, was because he was giving him failing grades. Ike would be staying at his place over the weekend, but kept it to himself. Fraternization between students and teachers was frowned upon.

Dr. Karl Heinemann was born a Lutheran in one of the numerous German colonies that dotted the rural landscape of Ukraine before the Revolution. His innate talents as a musician and linguist were honed at the University of Berlin where he studied theology and the cello. After a few years, he aban-

123

doned theology, and its ancient languages, to concentrate on music. It was a career that would take him to the concert stages of Odessa, Kiev, Moscow and St. Petersburg. And, it was in the pre-revolutionary capital, as a cellist with the St. Petersburg Opera Orchestra, where the Bolshevik Revolution overtook him, tearing the very heart and soul out of his career, and his life.

Two years earlier, while visiting his parents, he had met and fallen in love with Elfrieda Hiebert, a Mennonite girl from a neighbouring village. Her father had agreed to the marriage on condition that young Karl join the Mennonite Brethren Church. He dutifully did so, allowing himself to be rebaptized. His father-in-law to be had nodded in approval when Karl described his conversion, but showed mild disappointment that it had been a quiet one without drama or emotion.

It was a brief and tragic marriage. The Revolution brought famine and disease with it. It was the latter, in the form of typhus, that made Karl Heinemann a widower at the age of 29, and a fugitive from the rabid anti-Germanism gripping a nation in social and political turmoil. His flight ended as a hired hand on a Saskatchewan farm, where pitch forks and the reins of plow horses raised calluses on hands that had once brought the notes of Vivaldi and Boccharini to life on the concert stages of Russia.

In 1930, the first full year of the Great Depression, he moved to Winnipeg. Here, he gave cello lessons to the few who could afford them, and for a time played with the Winnipeg Symphony, a position with a lot of prestige but little money. There was no demand whatsoever for his proficiency in Hebrew and Greek until 1945, when the Bible School at Altbach added the two languages to its curriculum.

When the first teacher, with impeccable Christian credentials, was found to be badly out of his depth, the board called Dr. Heinemann. He was one of the very few authentic academics bible schools hired. When they did so, it was more out of necessity than dedication to higher standards of learning. So, every Monday morning during the fall and winter, he left his slightly seedy neighborhood off Portage Avenue, and walked the six blocks to the bus depot for the one hour trip to Altbach. Every Tuesday evening he caught the Winnipeg bus out of Altbach for the return trip. And, it was in Altbach where Ike and Dr. Heinemann met.

At first, Ike had found him to be even more reserved than the other teachers. He conducted his classes with an aloofness that camouflaged a basically shy nature. He invited few confidences. His lectures stuck to the topic at hand, specifically the nuts and bolts of the languages his charges were there to learn. If any student expected to get tips on how to use this knowledge to concoct catchy attention grabbing sermons, he was out of luck with Dr. Heinemann.

Ike might never have narrowed this distance between student and teacher, if it hadn't been for what he initially thought was a slip of the tongue. Perhaps he hadn't heard correctly. The other students obviously hadn't been listening at all, so after class he intercepted his teacher at the door.

"Dr. Heinemann, did you refer to, perhaps I misunderstood, but didn't you refer to the mythology of the Old Testament?"

"Perhaps you should frame your question in the context in which I used that word," Dr. Heinemann answered coolly.

"Well, the part where you were talking about the persecution of the Jews after the Crusades, and how they turned to the mythology and mysticism of Hebrew literature, especially the Old Testament."

"Maybe I should have stuck with the word `mysticism'. It's much safer, don't you think?" He gave Ike an enigmatic smile before picking up the conversation again. "I frequently see you on the Winnipeg bus. Next time, why don't we have a little talk; pass the time a bit."

"Sure. I'd like that," Ike replied, somewhat surprised. Unlike many of the other students, Ike did not find Dr. Heinemann boring, nor unspiritual for that matter. He wasn't even sure what was meant by the word. If Dr. Heinemann was something of a loner, he more than made up for it with unfailing politeness. And, it was his civility in dealing with his students and the other teachers that impressed Ike. While he invariably buried his head in a book or a newspaper the minute he sat down in the bus, he always had a quick smile and a friendly hello for every student he encountered.

During the first few trips, after the doorway conversation, Dr. Heinemann chatted amiably with Ike, but the words mythology and mysticism were never mentioned. Nor was anything remotely connected with Altbach Bible School. Ike had the feeling that Dr. Heinemann was genuinely interested in his growing up years at Kirkcaldy, his experiences with the draft board, the war, and his time with the Allied Occupation Forces in Germany. He was particularly interested in the latter, shaking his head in disbelief when Ike described the devastation of his beloved Berlin, where he had spent his halcyon days as a student. Yet, all the while, Ike had the unmistakable impression that Dr. Heinemann was taking his measure, gauging the zealousness of his faith and his intellectual curiosity. Slowly, he loosened up.

On the third or fourth bus trip, Dr. Heinemann said, "Ike, next time you're in the city why don't you stay at my place. I don't get many visitors. Besides, we've still got some mythology and mysticism to clear up, haven't we?"

Dr. Heinemann's "place" was a snug apartment on the second floor of one of those weathered Victorian houses that grace tree-lined streets in older sections of North American cities. They stand like aging dowagers putting the best face possible on genteel poverty. Built before the days of central heating, every level boasted a fireplace.

The fire, floor to ceiling shelving laden with books and classical recordings, the understated wall paper, all gave Dr. Heinemann's apartment a warm, if cluttered, ambience that invited thought and stimulating conversation. It was in stark contrast to the white wallboard sterility of the homes of the other teachers where bookshelves, if there were any, were thinly populated, and a morocco leather bound Bible was prominently displayed on the coffee table.

Ike walked to a corner of Dr. Heinemann's living room where a cello leaned on its stand, silent testimony to its owner's life long love affair with music. Ike ran his fingers lightly over its richly textured wood.

"It's a beautiful instrument," Ike said admiringly, by way of making small talk, while his host busied himself making coffee in the tiny kitchen.

"Yes, but I'm afraid it's second best. I lost my first cello during the Revolution. Losing your first instrument is like losing your real, first love. Maybe it's all in my head, but the music is

126

never quite the same again. I replaced my cello, but not my first love."

"Do you still play?" Ike asked.

"Not really. Just a bit with my students. Fingers too stiff." He splayed the fingers of both hands holding them up in Ike's direction. "Hurts even when I do this," he said.

"Do you miss playing, I mean concerts, that sort of thing?"

"Oh, yes. But it was time. You know, for a musician, giving up performing is a kind of death. "And," he said smiling, "it is important to die well."

Teacher and student settled themselves into well worn armchairs sipping coffee as black as Manitoba top soil. Dr. Heinemann spoke as if delivering a monologue, but animatedly, as lonely people often do. His conversation was wide ranging. He was pleased that Mennonites were beginning to embrace the truly great religious music of composers like Handel, Brahms and Haydn. He deplored the mindless little gospel ditties the churches were importing from the fundamentalist American South at the expense of the traditional Mennonite and Lutheran hymns.

He reminisced about his youth in Russia and his student days in Germany where he had once heard Albert Einstein give a lecture entitled, "Celestial Clockwork."

Abruptly, he switched from past to present tense, as if he had suddenly snapped out of a hypnotic trance. "Well, let's get to what concerns you," he said, focusing his pale blue eyes on Ike. "Biblical mythology, if I remember right."

"Yes, you seemed to suggest in one of your lectures that the Old Testament is really a mixture of Hebrew history, legend and mythology. Doesn't this go against our doctrine of faith?"

Dr. Heinemann frowned, bringing his long bony fingers together to form a small tent. Peering over the tops of his glasses, he studied them for a moment, then pressed the tips to his lips. "Why stop at the Old Testament?" he asked without looking up.

Speaking softly, he gave his analysis and interpretation of New Testament teaching as a continuum of the imagery and primitive mythology of the Old. Were such heresy to become known, it would have meant Dr. Heinemann's immediate dismissal from his teaching position, and loss of church member-

127

ship. So why, Ike wondered was he confiding in him of all people; someone half his age? Was Dr. Heinemann an agnostic? or heaven forbid an out and out atheist? Soon enough the conversation shifted to that very subject.

"If you were to ask me, and I know you are wondering, whether I am an atheist, I would answer with an emphatic no."

Relieved, Ike shifted in his chair. His personal doubts aside, he would have felt betrayed if his favorite teacher, and now mentor, turned out to be an atheist.

"Next question." Dr. Heinemann was speaking as he did in front of his class, posing a question, then answering it himself. "Next question. Am I an agnostic? Well, that depends on what you mean by that word. If by agnostic you mean that one cannot know God, then the answer is yes. If, on the other hand, you mean by agnostic someone who does not know whether or not there is a God, the answer is no." Sensing Ike's confusion, he proceeded to clarify his point.

"Do you recall me telling you that I once attended one of Einstein's lectures in Berlin?"

"Yes, the one about the clockwork in the cosmos?"

"Exactly. At that lecture, a student asked Einstein if there is a God, to which the famous physicist replied, `the question is not whether there is a God, but rather what kind of a God is there.'"

"Obviously," Ike said, "he doesn't believe in the God of the Jews we are taught to believe in."

"No, I don't think he does," Dr. Heinemann sighed.

Both men stared into the fire for some time, saying nothing. Finally Dr. Heinemann broke the silence. "What are your plans, still thinking of the ministry?"

"I'm having second thoughts. What do you think I should do?"

"Well," Dr. Heinemann laughed, "how clear was the call?" Ike smiled sheepishly. He couldn't bring himself to admit that this whole ministry business had been his mother's idea all along.

"I'm reluctant to advise you on that score, Ike. In one way, you'd make a fine preacher. I've noticed that you've learned to think on your feet, and your speaking skills have improved tremendously."

"You said `in one way' I'd make a good preacher, does that

mean in another I wouldn't?"

"Depends on whether you can come to terms with your doubts; more importantly, whether you are able to avoid falling into the trap so many of our ministers fall into."

"And, what's that?"

Dr. Heinemann didn't answer right away, as if he regretted having raised the subject, and when he did answer it was in a round about way. "Just remember this Ike, if you decide to take up preaching, go into it to do something, not be something."

Again, both men fell silent, staring into the fire. "Hypnotizing, isn't it?" Dr. Heinemann said, breaking the silence. Ike nodded, "I'm not used to an open fire in a house. We just had a wood burning heater back on the farm." Dr. Heinemann got up and tapped the spine of a slender volume among the row of books on a shelf. "An American philosopher, Henry Thoreau, had something to say about stoves and fireplaces. It was his opinion that fire in a stove is merely a chemical process. In a fireplace it's poetry."

Involuntarily Ike's gaze returned to the fire, as if expecting an ancient oracle of unquestioned authority to suddenly dispense infallible wisdom. Without taking his eyes off the flames, and sounding as though he was talking to himself, he said, "I've pretty well decided to get a teaching certificate. The ministry is not for me. Come to think of it, neither is the church."

"Don't give up the church lightly." Dr. Heinemann spoke slowly and deliberately. "There's more involved than just abandoning an institution. The Mennonite church is your root system. Your people's history, ethnicity, values, and yes, your inner being are bound up in it. Leave it, and you will spend the rest of your life trying to straddle two chairs."

"What you seem to be saying, Dr. Heinemann, is that there is no way of being a Mennonite, that is, identifying intimately with our culture and values, without believing in our theology."

"Essentially, yes. That is what I'm saying. But discarding the theology isn't as easy as you might think either. Whether you are aware of it or not, a strand of that faith will always remain deep in your psyche, and chances are that in some crisis, be it financial, the loss of a family member, or the moment you are staring your own death in the face, you will grasp that strand like a drowning man grabbing a life line."

The fire was nearly out. Only a scattering of gemlike embers glowed in a pile of ashes. Dr. Heinemann spread them with a poker to extinguish what remained of the fire, sending a shower of sparks through the open draft.

"Before we turn in," Dr. Heinemann said, "let me leave you with a final thought. Don't throw away good customs and traditional values, even a faith that turns out to be based on mythology and mysticism, unless you can replace them with something of value."

All sorrows can be borne if we tell a story about them

— Isak Denisen

THE BRIDGE

John felt good. The herringbone tweed jacket bought off the rack at Goodales Men's shop molded his spare shoulders as if tailored on Savile Row. The grey slacks matched perfectly and the ox-blood loafers comfortably accommodated his long, narrow feet.

He had debated with himself whether to check into a hotel before buying the new outfit, or shop first. He decided on the latter. The new clothes would make a better impression at the check-in desk at the Montclair. He had chosen the Montclair, not because it was the best hotel in Winnipeg, which it wasn't, but because it was upscale enough to discourage rural folk he might know from staying there.

The Fort Garry and the Royal Alexandra were more elegant but, he thought, there were better things to spend money on than tipping some toady dressed in a ridiculous Dickensian costume for opening doors he was quite capable of opening himself. And, having ventured briefly into the "Alex", as that hotel was affectionately known, he felt uncomfortable approaching its funereal registration desk where solemn clerks shuffled about like priests conducting high mass. Then, there would be the inevitable question, "And you have a reservation, sir?" John didn't have one.

Although he knew he could never be a part of their world, he pretended to belong with the people coming and going through the lobby on what appeared to be matters of pressing importance. There were grey-suited businessmen with angular Anglo Saxon noses poised above Clark Gable mustaches carrying bulging briefcases, small clutches of matronly women in navy blue dresses, close fitting hats and white gloves, leaving faint trails of perfume in their wake. John had no desire to actually get to know these people, just to bask in their proximity. Yes, this should have been his world that through some unfortunate twist of fate he had been denied.

John sank deeper into the boat-sized bathtub luxuriating in the hot water pouring from its enormous spout. From his half-prone position he could see his room reflected in the mirror and the carnations he had bought on impulse at the main floor florist shop. The lavender fragrance of the soap, the crimson blur of flowers in the fogged up mirror shimmering like a Monet painting, the glass of Jack Daniel's resting on the rim of the tub, all gave John a serene sense of well being.

Except for his mother's mild chokecherry wine, he had never tasted alcohol before, and didn't know one liquor from another. But he had, years before, seen an advertisement for Jack Daniel's in *Esquire* at his sister Sarah's place. Sarah had worked as a domestic for a well-to-do Winnipeg family before marrying a local farmer. She had brought a stack of old magazines with her. These John had devoured from cover to cover. He found the colored ads particularly interesting - shiny new automobiles with white walled tires parked in front of ivy-covered stone mansions; men in tuxedos with glamorous, long-gowned women on their arms. In some ads they were sipping champagne on the decks of ocean liners with the night skyline of a big city behind them. It was incomprehensible to John that there actually were people in the world who lived like that.

One beautiful ad that had somehow left an indelible impression on his consciousness showed a bottle of Jack Daniel's standing beside a large bouquet of red carnations.

When John had handed the down at heels gentleman on North Main a dollar with the promise of more if he could find a bootlegger for him, he had politely asked John in impeccable English, "And what is your pleasure young man?" Instinctively John had answered, "Jack Daniel's." The man's face crinkled into a toothless smile. "Not much call for that around here. See what I can do," he said, as he shuffled off.

As the sipping whiskey bit pleasantly into his throat, John drifted into a reverie of detachment from the misery he had left behind. He sat motionless, resting his head on the tiled wall behind him, all the while creating mental images of the activities planned for the days ahead.

Tomorrow night, a show. His first honest-to-goodness movie ever. The John Deere machinery films his parents reluctantly allowed him to watch at the Odd Fellows Hall didn't count. This would be a real movie in a real theatre with soft seats. The movie he had chosen was *Casablanca* brought back to a grubby little theatre near where he'd bought the Jack Daniel's.

John had once read in the *Free Press Prairie Farmer* that it was a good movie that had won three prizes called Oscars. He couldn't recall the name Bogart, but felt he had a degree of familiarity with Ingrid Bergman. He had read a feature on the stunningly beautiful Swedish actress in *Esquire.*

On Wednesday, it would be supper at Childs' Restaurant - white linen, real flowers on the table. Then later, a coffee at Molly's place, the friendly young woman in the pink high heels who had introduced herself when he was making the Jack Daniel's purchase and, who John assumed, had taken a fancy to him.

The next night, the first concert of the season by the Winnipeg Symphony. A violinist from New York, whose name John couldn't pronounce, would be performing. He knew next to nothing about classical music or its pantheon of famous composers. Yet, it was the kind of music that spoke so eloquently to his spirit. It was the swell of the string section that, at least for the moment, swallowed up the hurts and ugliness of his life. He listened to it on WGN Chicago whenever the reception was good, and there was no one else in the house. His parents considered it so much ungodly noise and made him turn if off whenever they caught him listening to it.

John drained the last drop of whiskey from the glass and slipped deeper into a mood of benevolent lethargy. He made a futile attempt at making a mental calculation of how long his money would last, but his mind kept drifting. His euphoria soon dissolved into a sound sleep.

John's trip to the city hadn't been planned. Monday had, until late in the afternoon, passed as usual; a replica of a thousand days before spent in the claustrophobic atmosphere of his family's farm - a place where a barn was always in need of cleaning and a house where plaster of paris bible plaques edged with brightly painted sprigs of daisies and violets looked down from every wall. Only the J.I. Case calender, with its idyllic blue mountain stream cascading over massive grey rocks, suggested that God may have created a beautiful world just for its own sake. Even here, John's mother decided that a picture without a religious connotation could only be justified if it was given a Christian imprint. On the largest rock she had placed one of her innumerable stickers

"...let the one who is thirsty come; let the one who wishes take the water of life without cost." Rev. 22:17

She got the little stickers, and a host of other scriptural knick-knacks from the Safe Harbour Radio Ministries for sending in love offerings. The kitchen kerosene lamp bore an oily, but still readable verse from Psalm 1:19 - *Thy word is a lamp unto my feet.* The rear licence plate of the aging family Chev was framed in reflective red reminding others on the road that "Jesus Saves." If there was a place in the house, or an object that didn't preach its own sermonette, it was only because they were awaiting the appropriate verse.

John was a worry to his mother. Of all her seven children only John was, well - different. Even strange. "John has never been like the other children," she confided to her spinster sister, Justina. "He takes down the bible verses I put up over his bed and doesn't pray at family devotions."

"He's seventeen now, isn't he?" Justina asked, knowing full well how old John was.

"Yes, last month."

"And he hasn't been saved yet? He hasn't given his heart to Jesus?" Justina clucked with feigned concern.

"No, I'm afraid not," John's mother sighed, wiping away a tear with the palm of her hand. "All he's interested in is reading books that shouldn't even be allowed in the house and listening to that noise on the radio."

"Maybe you've been too hard on him," Justina interjected in a solicitous manner. Her sister cast her a quizzical look.

"I mean," Justina quickly replied, "You did beat him pretty hard when he was small."

"Yes, but that isn't the problem. If anything, he didn't get enough discipline. In a Christian home, children can't be coddled." John's mother smeared another tear across her cheek. She cried easily.

"Yes," she went on, "my man is so weak-kneed he would never give John a good licking when he needed it."

"Well," said Justina, "the nail that sticks up must certainly be hammered down, but he's too big for you now."

"I leave it to Walter. He's such a good son. If anyone can straighten John out it's Walter."

Walter was John's only brother, ten years his senior. The situation between them had gone from bad to worse. When they were younger, Walter took a perverse pleasure in reporting

John's every misdeed to his mother. Now, he was taking matters into his own hands. As much as possible, John kept a safe distance from his brother. But to live up to the conduct expected of him would have tried the piety of a saint.

The day John made his fateful decision was a blistering hot one, the sun's laser-like rays cast a suffocating pall of lethargy over plant, beast and man. It was unusual weather for the last week of August. John finished hoeing and mounding the last row of wilting potatoes and took momentary refuge from the heat in the relative coolness of the kitchen. The eight day Westclox alarm on the stove showed ten minutes to five. At five, he would have to get on his pony and fetch the cows for milking. He sat down heavily, cradling his head in his crossed arms spread over the table and dozed off.

Suddenly the screen door sprang open awakening John with a start. It was twenty minutes past five. He had overslept. Walter stood in the doorway holding the riding reins with the steel bit attached. John rose groggily from the table. Walter swung the bit like an ancient warrior wielding a spiked ball and chain. It struck John full force in the small of the back. Before he could regain his balance, another blow cut across his shoulders, then another. John groped at the bit, but managed only to deflect it toward the back of his skull. He felt a wet, warm trickle run into his shirt collar. The kitchen swam before his eyes, then everything went black.

John opened his eyes to find Walter bent over him whimpering, "Is he dead? Is he dead?" His mother, standing in the door, arms loosely folded over her apron replied, "He'll be alright. But next time Walter, not so hard."

"There won't be a next time Mother. Never." John's words came out hard and cold, each drawn from a well of hatred, the depths of which even he was unaware existed until that moment. "There will never, never, be a next time."

John went outside and carried out his assigned chores like a sleepwalker. He brought the cows in from the south pasture, milked those allotted to him, slopped the pigs and turned the sweat encrusted work horses into the night pasture. Before supper, which he declined to eat, he took a dip in the cattle dugout to wash off the day's grime, and went straight to the bedroom he shared with his brother.

He faked a sound sleep when Walter came into the room. He didn't stir a muscle while his older brother said his prayers. John didn't look but he knew Walter was kneeling beside his bed as he always did, praying silently through moving lips.

When Walter's breathing became heavy and measured, John got up, put on his Sunday clothes and walked quietly downstairs. In the kitchen he pulled out a large drawer next to the butcher knives, lifted his father's thick accounts scribbler and removed an envelope which, he knew, held four hundred and fifty three dollars. That was the exact amount the teller at the Bank of Toronto had counted out in front of his father when he had cashed two grain cheques earlier in the week. John always acted as translator for his father, who spoke only German, whenever he did his banking.

John tugged his shirt collar over his neck against the rapidly cooling night air. The road leading from the farm house stretched before him like a luminescent ribbon under a nearly full moon.

An hour of brisk walking brought him to the railway overpass where he and his friends had, in their younger years, spent Sunday afternoons clambering over the girders at the lower ends of the bridge. Only George Epp had dared scale the steel framework to the top of the arch, and stand there spread-eagled while a freight hurtled through underneath him. He said he'd never do it again because the sudden updraft generated by the cinder-spewing engine had nearly made him lose his grip.

John put down his small suitcase and peered down from the railing to the creosote smelling rail line below. He leaned over a bit farther, and was able to make out the place where George had stood. He stared at the spot for a few moments before picking up his suitcase to continue his journey.

He got to the hard top at McDougal Corners and waited half an hour for the bus. He slipped comfortably into a soft seat. Almost of its own weight his head dropped onto the napkin-draped backrest.

The driver ground the gears into low and lurched onto the highway. Four hours away, the big city awaited. But all that had been a week ago.

Now, John sat staring at the wilted carnations. Loneliness hung over him like a heavy fog. He had managed to see

Casablanca, but hadn't made it to the symphony. He had gone to Childs' several times - with Molly, and had been amazed at the ravenous appetite of a woman with such a slender figure. Ah yes, Molly - her round white shoulders, lips ever so slightly parted, a storm of blonde curls topping an expectant twenty year old face illuminated by a street lamp outside her bedroom window. The light had softened a hardness already encroaching around her mouth and eyes.

Her clothes, John thought, were elegant. Every evening she emerged from her cluttered and clothing-strewn room like a gorgeous butterfly breaking free from its chrysalis. John was certain she could hold her own anywhere, and wouldn't have looked out of place at a table next to Ingrid Bergman sipping cocktails at Rick's Cafe Americain in *Casablanca*. Like Bogart, Ingrid's tough guy lover, he too would sacrifice anything for his woman. And like Bogart, he had been generous. So generous that the money he'd given Molly, and the meals at Childs' had left him nearly broke. Although he held back enough to check out of the Montclair, there wasn't enough left to move into cheaper accommodation and look for a job.

He spread out the money he had left on the table, and pushed aside the amount needed to pay the hotel bill. He counted the remainder. There was enough for bus fare back to McDougal Corners and five dollars for Molly. She wanted the money so her sick mother could fill a prescription. She had so much wanted to see John off at the bus depot but simply had "a hundred and one things to do". Would John be a darling and just slip the money under her door?

It was nearly midnight when the Greyhound rumbled off the pavement onto the gravelled approach at McDougal Corners. John let his eyes adjust to the inky blackness before starting for home. Every mile or so an anemic light blinked from a distant farm house, but the lateness of the hour assured him that road traffic was unlikely.

In the darkness, the overpass bridge John knew so well looked sinister and foreboding. Like a pre-historic monster it crouched over the railway tracks. John's thoughts were not on the bridge, but what lay a short distance beyond; the sour smell of milk pails, dung-caked milk cows, fly-specked windows, and a place where violent discipline passed for love. Exactly how he would be received he did not know. Of one thing he was certain. There would no fattened calf killed to celebrate his homecoming.

Once on the bridge, John stopped. He pulled out his pocket watch, but couldn't make out the time. He estimated it was well past two. The east bound freights would soon start coming through at regular intervals.

Without any particular thought in his head he walked to the lower end of the bridge and began climbing the girders hand over hand, leg over leg, to the point where he had stopped as a child. He paused briefly, then continued towards the spot where George had nearly been blown off by the force of a passing train. The only thought that now went through his mind was that his nearly new loafers were most unsuitable for traversing steel girders.

As he took the last steps to the high point, soft flashes of light began dancing in lovely patterns across the network of supports and on the backs of his hands. He carefully turned to face the light which had now become blindingly bright, pushed forward by a low, steady rumble.

John loosened his grip on one hand, then the other, letting himself fall into a black cauldron of cinders, scalding steam, and pounding steel. The force catapulted him over an abyss and into the unfathomable depths of quiet non-being.

The earth does not belong to man.
Man belongs to the earth

— Chief Seattle

SPIRIT OF DELIGHT

There's something to be said for growing up a country boy. Actually, there's a lot to be said for it. The poet got it right when he wrote, "God made the country, man made the town."

Where I grew up, He made lots of land and sky, but skimped on the water. Nevertheless, every spring a network of creeks that fed the Assiniboine River sprang to life with the sprightliness and saucy dash of a mountain stream. Within a few weeks their newfound energy exhausted itself. They reverted to their sluggish former self, or dried up completely. But not before replenishing a string of sloughs in their path. These would soon be dignified by pairs of mating mallards, serenaded by choruses of frogs...those vocal barometers of environmental health. Again, the creeks had fulfilled their purpose of carrying on the work started millennia before by the continental ice cap, whose melt molded river beds and carved the graceful, round shouldered valleys.

The beauty of the landscape wasn't the heart-stopping kind to be found farther west. If the towering canyons of the Rockies are the cathedrals of the human spirit, then the furrowing hills, hard by our prairie farm, represented the little brown church in the vale.

A straight line of poplars, tall and white trunked, had stationed themselves like soldiers between the road allowance and the place of my childhood pleasures. They stood erect and uncompromising, as if to say to the encroaching world, `this far and no farther'.

My enchantment with this little prairie oasis was not generally shared. I once persuaded my Sunday School teacher to hold our annual picnic there instead of on someone's farm yard. But, the area farmers saw it as a wasteland where nature had cheated them out of arable land. To make matters worse, the stunted grass and ubiquitous bluffs made it unsuitable for grazing.

But, in my childish fantasies, I saw herds of snorting buffalo charging into the trees to escape the black flies, and copper-skinned Cree hunters camped in the clearings. And, not so many years before, that had actually been the case. Sides of boulders were still smooth from countless generations of buffalo rubbing off their winter accumulation of mangy shag. And, the occasional arrowhead could still be found in sandy spots exactly where they had been lost by Indian hunters hundreds of years before.

The area, no more than a few hundred acres, was an appendage to what we called the `Big Bush' to the north. It became my second home. In retrospect, perhaps it was my first home. Nothing in my life was as magical, nothing before or since has brought me so close to my Creator. Long before I read, or even heard, of Shelley, I felt the inner vibrations of his `Song'.

> *I love all that thou lovest,*
> *Spirit of Delight!*
> *The fresh Earth in new leaves*
> *dressed,*
> *And the starry night;*
> *Autumn evening, and the morn*
> *When golden mists are born.*
>
> *I love snow, and all the forms*
> *of the radiant frost;*
> *I love waves, and wind, and storms,*
> *Every thing almost*
> *Which is Nature's and may be*
> *Untainted by man's misery.*

After a heavy rain, I swam in a small pond a few hundred yards beyond the row of guardian poplars. It wasn't until a colony of beavers built a dam that the water stayed deep enough to swim in all summer. Here, garter snakes slipped through the tall slough grass that edged the water. It was my very own Walden's Pond where I could observe a micro world of water beetles etching paths across the still water, and sky blue dragon flies darting a few feet above as if inspecting their intricate handiwork.

Tangled copses on the sides of arching hills were alive with the whirring wings of warblers, percussionists to the virtuoso meadowlark whistling melodic notes from his perch on a distant fence post. All seemed to be endlessly tuning for some mighty symphony.

At dusk, amber columns of white tails, coaxed from shady glades by the promise of protective night, angled their way up steep hill sides to graze on the bench.

I have forgotten the names of most of the wild flowers that grew in the gullies and woods. But the wonder of them hasn't been forgotten, nor all of their names. There were the red-berried ferrybells, the brown-eyed susans, and Indian paints. The most prized of all were the waxy yellow lady slippers which, I always thought, looked more like Dutch wooden shoes than a lady's slipper. And, there were the masses of white snowdrops that sheltered in the shade of the poplar bluffs. By mid-August the blossoms, so recently in their prime, began to wither and fade, resigned to their fate. On the prairie giving birth is difficult, death is easy.

Year round, at a sharp bend in the main creek, I rested on a low wall of exposed limestone. In its layers of petrified time tiny fossilized sea shells and water insects lay entombed, speaking to me eloquently of creation's genesis.

This early exposure to the wonders of nature made an indelible impression on me. I realized that never having marvelled at the mystery and beauty of the world around us is a terrible thing for the soul. Nature itself is not God, but He may be found in every awesome and humble aspect of it if we but take time to look.

Like most country boys, I was often careless with nature. I hunted and trapped; killed things needlessly. I don't kill anymore. Long ago, I began to look critically on my own transgressions and all those who, in Thoreau's words, "speak of heaven and disgrace the earth".

Although nothing in my life has been as magical as those Elysian Fields of my youth, I have never gone back. Experience has taught me that it is not wise to revisit perfection.